EMBODIED LIGHT

HARIRI PONTARINI ARCHITECTS

EMBODIED LIGHT

THE BAHÁ'Í TEMPLE OF SOUTH AMERICA

BIRKHÄUSER
BASEL

"A servant is drawn unto Me in prayer until I answer him: and when I have answered him, I become the ear where-with he heareth..." For thus the Master of the house hath appeared within His home, and all the pillars of the dwelling are ashine with His light.

Bahá'u'lláh, *The Seven Valleys*

CONTENTS

Embodied Light evolved from a fateful meeting I had with editor Andreas Müller years ago at a steel conference in Hannover at which I was keynote speaker. Andreas suggested we put together this book, and I am grateful to him and the Birkhäuser team for their assistance and encouragement throughout the process.

Comprised of drawings, models, renderings, and full-colour panoramic photographs, this book showcases the technological innovation and architectural excellence of the Bahá'í Temple of South America. Douglas Martin, former member of the Universal House of Justice, contributed a foreword; writer and architectural critic Lisa Rochon penned an essay, William Thorsell, senior fellow at the Munk School of Global Affairs of the University of Toronto, led an interview with me; and visual artist Sky Glabush and scholar Robert Weinberg shared essays in honour of the project.

Embodied Light is intended to share the 14-year journey culminating in the opening of the last of the eight continental temples to be completed as part of a remarkable portfolio of sacred architecture commissioned by the Bahá'í Community. My hope is that readers will gain insights into our creative process, as well as the vision. This book is for architects, engineers, and designers, and for anyone interested in this journey. As with the Temple itself, it is an invitation to architectural and spiritual pilgrimage.

The sense of fairness, openness, and collaboration that pervaded the construction of this particular House of Worship has been incredible. Many people have been instrumental in completing the Temple in Chile, so we put together a separate Acknowledgements section at the back of this book. Here, I need to mention that I would not have submitted a design proposal were it not for the gentle nudging of my wife Sasha. As well, David Pontarini, my partner at Hariri Pontarini Architects, never wavered in his support, allowing our team the time and space to fully commit to the work.

Of course, all this was made possible with the guidance and unfailing support of The Universal House of Justice, including former members Hooper Dunbar, Douglas Martin, and Dr. Farzam Arbab, and current member Gustavo Correa, all of whom were influential in carrying out the House's vision. It's impossible to communicate the privilege and bounty my team and I felt working directly with the House of Justice, and as a Bahá'í, it was a very special experience for me.

Siamak Hariri
Toronto, September 2017

FOREWORD

One of the major undertakings pursued on a global level by the Bahá'í community has been the construction of centres of worship. The program began with establishing central 'Houses of Worship' to serve each continent. Building national and local Temples of this sort is now also underway.

The final structure in the continental series is that of South America, the site chosen being Santiago, Chile. For several years I had the privilege of serving on the international governing body of the Bahá'í community, the Universal House of Justice. By happy coincidence, I was appointed, with two of my colleagues, to a committee to review a design for the Chile House of Worship. We had received some 180 submissions of proposals, of a wide range of appropriateness, from all over the world. My colleagues and I widdled the applicants down to four, whose creators were then asked to submit fully detailed designs. In the process, Siamak Hariri's submission stood alone as a brilliant piece of work, a submission that required only one brief session to win a unanimous decision of the Faith's governing institution.

The Bahá'í Faith is, at its heart, a religion of unity in diversity, based on recognition that the human race has reached the stage of its maturity. In the words of the Faith's founder, Bahá'u'lláh, "the earth is but one country and mankind its citizens." The mission of the Bahá'í community is to give active meaning to this profound truth, in all aspects of its work.

Services in places of Bahá'í worship have no sermons, no man-made hymns, no instrumental music. Programs consist of readings from all of the world's religions and the nine-sided Temple design requirement itself is a mirror on this conception. Rather than reflecting some mystical symbolism, the number nine, highest of the single digits, reminds visitors not only of the unity but also the equality of all of the revealed Faiths that have brought humanity to this stage in its evolution.

Magnificent gardens likewise reflect the limitless possibilities to which unity can give birth. In time, each House of Worship will serve as a spiritual centre for the fulfilment of these possibilities: auxiliary buildings designed to provide such services to the community as a clinic, a school, a library, and a residence for the elderly.

A metaphor that appears with particular frequency in the Bahá'í writings is 'light,' drawing attention always to the transforming power of unity. Inspired by unity, all things become both possible and appealing. It is not surprising, therefore, that every effort is made by the community to give expression to this spiritual principle in Bahá'í structures of many kinds and most particularly in the design of Houses of Worship.

Siamak's original idea was to use alabaster, splendid as it is luminous. However, after extensive initial testing, it became obvious that a structure created from it would not hold up to the demands of the Temple. Happily, Siamak discovered the genius of another highly original Torontonian, Jeff Goodman; working together they conceived a system of straight and curved glass panels, ideal for the needs of the House of Worship. Not only, therefore, is the Santiago Temple luminous and beautiful, but it realizes the possibilities of an essentially new building material.

In all that has been said here, I have neglected a related achievement of Siamak's that was not architectural but that succeeded in brilliantly serving architecture's goal. To my knowledge, none of the other magnificent buildings of the Bahá'í world required their architects to first search, identify, and negotiate acquisition of the properties involved. After months of effort and repeated setbacks in these respects, setbacks that would have severely undermined the confidence of outstanding professionals in his field, Siamak was able to secure for his architectural triumph the stage it required. The broad hill on which the Temple has been erected overlooks central Santiago stretched out below, and is itself dramatically presented against the towering curtain of the Andes spread out behind.

I am confident (and not alone in this view) that Siamak will, in time, come to be acknowledged as one of Canada's history-making architects. From a Canadian Bahá'í point of view, he has encouraging predecessors. In the early years of the twentieth century, William Sutherland Maxwell, a Montreal architect who, working as the designer in partnership with his brother Edward, could boast a series of some of Canada's most important buildings. Included among these are the central tower of the Château Frontenac in Quebec City, the Palliser Hotel in Calgary, Saskatchewan's parliamentary building, and the Montreal Museum of Fine Art. Toward the end of Sutherland's life he had the internationally hailed achievement of designing and supervising the erection of the Shrine of the Báb, towering above the city of Haifa in Israel. Yet another Canadian Bahá'í architect, Louis Bourgeois, was of similar renown in designing and supervising the erection of the continental Bahá'í House of Worship for North America. In the beauty of its design, its pioneering of new building material, and above all, the clarity of its spiritual message, it has achieved a unique architectural authority in the Chicago area.

With similar gifts, with similar originality, and similar courage, Siamak is following in the path.

Douglas Martin

MOVEMENT. LIGHT. ECSTASY.

LISA ROCHON

Original wing detail
sketch by Siamak Hariri
depicting the idea of
capturing light between
two layers — embodied
light.

Ecstasy in architecture comes from depth of memory and personal conviction. *Ek-stasis*, from the Ancient Greek, means "to put out of place." As with any great work of architecture, there are many ways to consider and interpret the Bahá´í Temple of South America: a Temple of light expressing a faith of inclusion; a place for spiritual contemplation and architectural pilgrimage; also, transporting, out of place — ecstatic.

Nearly 14 years in the making, the Chilean Temple by Canadian architect Siamak Hariri represents the last of the eight continental Temples to be completed as part of a global portfolio of landmark sacred architecture commissioned by the Bahá´í community.

Surrounded by reflecting pools and a landscape of native grasses, the Bahá´í Temple of South America is a domed, luminous structure that echoes the rolling topography of the Andes, while appearing to float some 30 metres above the earth. Its nine monumental glass veils frame an open and accessible worship space where up to 600 visitors can be accommodated on curved walnut and leather seating. Looking up to the central oculus at the apex of the dome, visitors will experience a mesmerizing transfer of light from the exterior of cast glass to an interior of translucent Portuguese marble.

Both spiritual and temporal realms are acknowledged and embraced. In his design quest for an ecstatic place of worship, Siamak has achieved a heroic kind of architecture that rejects conventional practice to favour pure vision. Honouring the curve, honouring the complexity of nature, rejecting the Cartesian grid. Here, there is a privileging of a disordered order from a light-infused skin collaged together with irregular shapes. More Helen Frankenthaler diaphanous paintings or Man Ray photo collage than De Stijl. None of the cladding parts repeat, the only repetition being nine identically shaped veils.

Le Corbusier is said to have "forged an immediate bond with the landscape"[1] when he first visited the top of a steep hill in the hardscrabble mining village of Ronchamp in northeastern France. There, he designed the Chapel of Notre-Dame-du-Haut (1954), which I consider to be one of the most powerful works of the twentieth century. Just as Le Corbusier did decades earlier, Siamak Hariri bonded with his site and listened to the acoustic of its landscape.

For years, the architect and his client conducted an exhaustive search for a site near Santiago that would offer an exhilarating and generous landscape in which visitors could be enveloped and transported by nature. Several sites were considered, and rejected. Finally, about 14 kilometres outside of Santiago, at a former golf course beyond a gated housing estate, Siamak walked alone across the foothills to stop, intuitively, it seemed, at a plateau framed by the monumental Andes. The sprawl of the city lay below. This site became the final destination for the Temple. Its transformation has been the product of a remarkable collaboration. The acclaimed Chilean landscape architect, Juan Grimm, has masterminded the reinvention of a barren golf course that, over time, will blossom into a lush, colourful landscape planted with native, drought-resistant varieties.

The design represents a template of painful and triumphant experimentation. When I first wrote about the Bahá'í Temple of South America in 2003 in *The Globe and Mail*, the competition-winning design featured an exterior of alabaster. I wrote about it again in my book, *Up North: Where Canada's Architecture Meets the Land* (2005) when the design was imagined for a different site near Colina, north of Santiago. Through years of experimentation, working with Jeff Goodman at his glass-making studio in Toronto, a new kind of material created by baking cast glass was innovated for the exterior skin. Luminous and white is what Siamak Hariri had in mind; seen up close, the Temple cladding evokes streams of milk or snowflakes frozen in place.

Significantly, the exterior cast-glass panels are stronger than stone, according to tests, to satisfy a Bahá'í requirement that the building endure for 400 years, and to survive one of the most active earthquake zones in the world.

Though the materials had changed, the fundamental vision for the Temple remained the same: that it should capture and channel light to honour a place of deep spiritual pilgrimage.

At its most sublime, spiritual architecture has always attempted to capture and liberate the light. Seen through the bluish-mauve stained glass of the north rose window of Notre Dame Cathedral in Paris, I have written previously, light appears to us like intelligence. At the chapel by Eero Saarinen at the Massachusetts Institute of Technology in Cambridge, light appears from a single, benevolent source at the top of the conical roof.

The transformative power, the *ek-stasis* of the design, occurs within the interior. Stepping inside for my first time, I became instantly convinced that the Chilean Temple will stand in the world as a place of deep spiritual experience. The Temple contains a rare spatial force, its exhilarating and monumental single room defined by nine seemingly spinning veils. Looking up to the apex of the dome with its countless faceted panels, it appears that the veils are actually feathers and they are knotted — in marble — at the top. The whole is suffused with a mediated light, in tones that range from silver to grey to cream, and that shift to gold and ochre as the sun prepares to set in the evening.

In 2016, when Siamak and I flew to Santiago to visit the Temple, I experienced for the first time the epic sweep of the Andes, and, in contrast, the modesty of the Temple gesture. In this scenario, architecture cannot compete with this scale of nature — a humbleness suggested by Siamak's earliest watercolours of his Temple design. Just as the Andes rise and fall according to their trajectory or fade

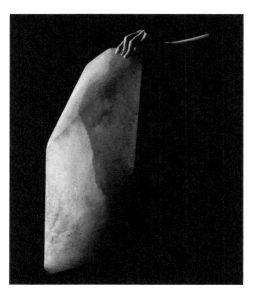

Light 'kissing' a piece of alabaster.

away during heavy mist, the Temple, too, can recede from the eye. When I first climbed the hill toward the Temple, walking up the stairs with the bronze handrail and along the sweep of a curved path, a landscaped berm hid the structure from my view. Instead, I was surrounded by the sweep of the newly planted native shrubs and trees and, in the distance, the magnificence of the Andes. Only when the path turned a corner was I re-introduced to the Temple, its volume shimmering in a long reflecting pool.

As is the case with all of the continental Temples around the world, a dome was an integral requirement handed to Siamak's team. The dome is a part of nature, and the human form. The dome defines the igloo of the Canadian north and the stupas of India. They are the shape of African huts and the Roman Pantheon commissioned by the emperor Hadrian. The dome has defined the architectural magnificence of the sixteenth-century Duomo cathedral by Filippo Brunelleschi in Florence; and, the Hagia Sophia — some 1,400 years old — in Istanbul. For the Bahá'í House of Worship, the dome has been interpreted as a complex curved structure enlivened by movement and accessibility to all peoples.

Openness and transparency are fundamental to both the structure and its site. It is critical to emphasize that all faiths are welcome within this House of Worship for prayer and meditation. Without ritual or clergy, without icons or images, Bahá'í Temples are conceived to reflect an ideal of universal worship where women, men, and children can gather together as equals. Many thousands lined up for the opening of the Temple in October 2016. For those lucky enough to visit in the future, an experience of *ek-stasis* awaits them.

---

1   Ezra Stoller, *The Chapel at Ronchamp* (New York: Princeton Architectural Press, 1999), p. 3.

WILLIAM THORSELL

Original sketch by
Siamak Hariri exploring
the idea of movement
around a centre.

In the spring of 2016, William Thorsell met with Siamak Hariri in the Toronto office
of Hariri Pontarini Architects to discuss the genesis of The Bahá'í Temple of South
America; the challenges of creating a new form of sacred space with no patterns
or models to draw from; and the abundance of cooperation that pervaded the
work, at every stage of its realization.

**William Thorsell: What is the core precept of the Bahá'í Faith? Who are the
Bahá'ís?**

Siamak Hariri: In the Bahá'í Faith, worship is not isolated; it is embedded in one's
daily life. Worship goes hand-in-hand with daily service, daily work, and daily
practice. It is the inhale and your daily life becomes the exhale. Bahá'u'lláh[1] has
proclaimed all religions are one. I like to use the analogy of nesting dolls. Imagine
a set of nesting dolls: each religion nests on the previous one. Only man has
separated these things. Fundamentally, the Bahá'í Faith is about the unity of all
religions and the unity of all mankind.

How do you characterize a Bahá'í House of Worship, or a Mashriqu'l-Adhkár?

As an architect, to try to design a *Mashriqu'l-Adhkár* in the early days of the Faith
is not easy. It was exciting, but also frightening, because this was such a new type
of building. The program was deceptively simple — a sacred, circular structure,
with nine sides, welcoming and embracing people from all walks of life, all
backgrounds, all religions, or no religion at all. This is a single room — a place of
worship — where there is no pulpit and no clergy. In these divisive times, when
the world is putting up walls, the design needed to express, in form, the very
opposite. It needed to be inclusive, and welcoming to all. A new type of sacred
space in the annals of religion. One without recipe or precedent. And, of course,
we are in the early days of the Faith, so it was like designing a church at the advent
of Christianity.

**Can you talk about how you and your client found each other and the critical
birth-moment of the project?**

Put simply, it was a call for designs — a competition to create a Bahá'í House of
Worship in South America. Two weeks before the deadline, my wife Sasha nudged
me into submitting. The Universal House of Justice received 180 submissions
from over 80 countries. It was a two-staged process, so they reduced it to four

teams, and then gave us four months to button-down our design. They had a very clear budget, so we had to reduce ours by 15 per cent. Just before the final decision, they asked if there was something we'd like to change. I did not realize this, but once they announced the design, there would be no re-visiting of that aspect. We had this mandate to then execute it and get it built. So, I said, "Yes, actually, we had designed it 15 per cent larger for very specific reasons." We wanted it to be exactly the same height as the Shrine of the Báb in Haifa, which has a majestic scale but also this extraordinary intimacy. If any building can hold the mountain, *that* building can hold a mountain. At the same time, you feel like you can nestle into it. That's a very difficult combination. So they agreed.

Sketch by Siamak Hariri.

How did you face the challenge of creating a form that would be universally welcoming and attractive?

It did not come quickly. We had four months, and the first two months were a series of experiments. We felt like we were in a deep dark place. I reflect back on our design process, and it reminds me of the story of Majnun, the crazy lover, who is crawling on his hands and knees digging around in the dirt. Someone asks him what he's doing, and he says, "I'm looking for Layli, I'm looking for my beloved." Then Majnun hits the wall, and has to climb it. This was our process. It was a fervent search, and we had to experiment, to go through a kind of controlled abandon. I liken it to falling backwards, and you hope that the process catches you.

Then, accidents started to happen as we evolved the form, and eventually, because we were combining the latest technology with these handcrafted models, the idea sprang from an intuition, a feeling. It wasn't form. I call it 'embodied light' because of this wonderful passage in the Bahá'í writings describing prayer: "A servant is drawn unto Me in prayer until I answer him ..." It's a fascinating relationship. Not every prayer is answered. If his prayer is answered, his very being becomes embodied light.[2] Your very being becomes "ashine" with His light.

So, I drew this sketch of something with two translucent and light layers, with a structure in between. It was a pure form — dome-like — but it ended up looking too much like an egg.

We continued to explore the idea of light being captured — embodied — somehow catalyzed within the material structure of the Temple. To create a building alive with light, we invented this new material utilizing cast glass, which takes light and absorbs it. The structure also has translucent stone on the inside. When it receives just a kiss of light, a prayer is answered, and the whole piece of stone comes alive. The light does not go through it, but becomes captured within the membrane.

I remember watching this beautiful video made by a five-year-old, about what plants do when you move the light. This is an apt metaphor for what prayer can do. It's so simple, but it has the magic of what a great temple will do. Somehow the architecture should express this idea of reach and movement towards the light, and, in the case of a temple, towards the heavens and the Divine. We wanted to express movement, as well as soft forms, in the way that a structure can embrace you.

Early Maya model
showing the soft ethereal
lines of the Temple.

Your vision for the Temple sprang from an intuition, a feeling. Intuition means that you are swimming in the values and aspirations of a particular group for a long enough time. And intuition starts to lead you towards expression.

From the beginning, I believe we felt we were guided. Maybe you can call that intuition. It was a struggle, not an immediate thunderbolt, for sure.

You have to swim and you have to make many ugly, bad mistakes. However, you know the difference between something that's interesting or promising, and something that is not. So, at each moment your intuition has to choose. You have to make the right decision.

That process does not stop the moment the design is chosen, because the extension of finding the right material and executing the design, live in conformity with the original design. The crafting of the building, the tectonics, the finding of the right site — all of that belongs to the same process that began with that earliest model.

As a Bahá'í, how have legacy and tradition informed your design process for this South America Temple?

In our family, we like to tell the story about my great great grandfather Qasim. He and his wife could not have a child, but they prayed to God for one, and their wish was granted. When my great grandmother Khanum Agha was born, her father put her on a scale, and then did the same with the equivalent of gold. Qasim was a builder, a great builder, and he went on horseback through Iraq to be with Bahá'u'lláh. He wanted to be with his soul's desire, but he was also there to give thanks for the child, with that offering of gold. Qasim offered to build something with his own hands, and that ended up being the summer room in the Ridván Garden, which is where pilgrims come to pray. This piece of family history stuck with me as I imagined a way to honour all that came before.

On both my mother's side and my father's side, many such stories exist. That's five generations' worth of stories of struggle and sacrifice. My father, the engineer, and my mother, the aesthete, made a beautiful pair. And having been born and raised in Germany and Switzerland, I developed a love of craft, which was complemented by a Persian sense of refinement.

Our design for the South American Temple should also honour the North American Mother Temple — the first Temple of Light, which is in Chicago. It's a masterpiece, so we had to aim high.

We didn't want to copy the old forms. It couldn't just look like a mosque or a synagogue or a cathedral, or an opera hall or an art gallery. It had to be pure unanticipated inspiration. We relied on the furthest reaches of what we knew, maybe to the realm of our dreams, aspiring for the ineffable qualities of sensuousness, and emotion. This takes me back to thirty years earlier, when I was studying architecture across the street from the art gallery designed by the great architect Louis Kahn. One day at the gallery, I saw the security guard run his hand across the concrete wall in appreciation. I could see, from the expression on his face, that he was moved by the building and that architecture could move the spirit, eliciting an emotional response. There was no prescription, and there were almost no restrictions in designing this new structure. In search of a 'feeling,' we looked outside of architecture, to organic forms and to art for inspiration and universality: a cheekbone; the veins of a leaf; the curve of a woven Japanese basket; the flow of a skirt of a whirling dervish; the calligraphic matrix of a Mark Tobey painting. We explored the idea of soft lines that would merge, like drapery, perhaps as nine translucent veils, folding and torqueing towards an apex. This was reminiscent of what we saw in the plant video.

So, you were intent on capturing this feeling of embodied light, but when did the definitive 'a-ha' moment occur?

The turning point was looking at the drawings of Louis Bourgeois, the architect of the Chicago Temple. Those drawing were 150 feet long! He started on one corner of the page and he would draw and draw for weeks. The commitment, the dedication, the love — this touched me. And it absolutely informed our vision for the Temple in Chile.

I also recall the story of the beloved Master, 'Abdu'l-Bahá,[3] when He laid the cornerstone for the Chicago Temple in 1912. 'Abdu'l-Bahá said to the friends gathered on that occasion, "The Temple is already built." It took 50 years for the community to build it; the architect, Bourgeois, died before it was completed.

The Bourgeois drawings put us in a certain mindset of how high the aspiration really was, helping us form a commitment that was 14 years in the making, for a Temple that would last 400 years.

Does the Temple really need to last 400 years?

Yes, the Universal House of Justice set up a design mandate for 400 years for the engineering of the building — a difficult and astounding design constraint, given that most institutions look no further than five years ahead. The Temple is located in a very active seismic zone. We had three universities working together, one in California, one in Chile, and one in Toronto. They devised a pendulum isolation system that would allow for 600 millimetres of movement, so that, in the event of an earthquake, the building would rock and return to the centre.

As you said, the nature of the whole vision required the invention of materials, as well as new engineering and structural approaches. Almost everything about this required something to be created.

It was an extraordinarily rich team effort. Every aspect of this, the people on our own team here, the project manager down in Chile, everybody played a very important role. It was like a well-functioning orchestra.

So, your team is working together and you are feeling the presence of something bigger propelling you forward. How much time did you spend with your client during this process?

The thing that was exceptional, in this case, was the client and the absolute,

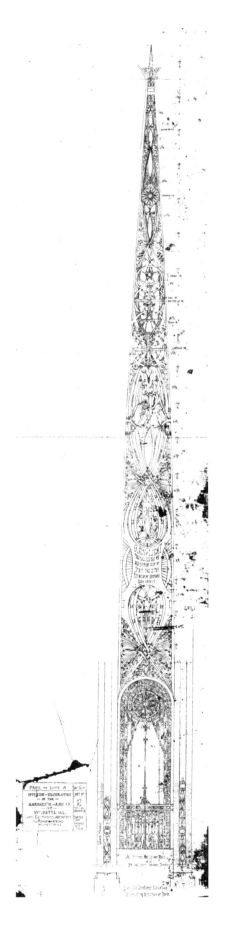

The Bahá'í Temple
of Light in Wilmette,
Illinois — the oldest
Bahá'í House of Worship
in the world.

Interior decoration
drawing for the
Mashriqu'l-Adhkár,
Wilmette, Illinois;
Louis Bourgeois; dated
July 27, 1928.

unwavering commitment, the sense of confidence that they gave everyone on
the project. In 14 years, there was never a disruptive moment. Additionally, they
gave the project the right time. There was always this sense that, "Oh, well this is
obviously going to take a little longer than we thought, but, it will ultimately reach
its goal." When that confidence comes from your client in a very calm manner,
you really do everything you can to succeed.

**A clear idea, one voice, one single point of contact, and decisive. It sounds like
that's that kind of client that you had.**
Yes. The spirit has been extraordinary, with both Gartner Steel and Glass and our
own team. Not one heated moment. I've never had that in 30 years. Secondly, it
was done with a sense of fairness and openness, knowing it was a team effort.
That spirit has pervaded throughout the various stages.

Usually there are surprises with complex projects. What were some of those?
We had very few surprises, but there were several obstacles. We were told it
would be impossible to build, impossible to stay on budget, and impossible to get a
site. We managed to stay within three per cent of our budget, but it took nine years
to find the site. During those years of searching, we got the drawings, engineering,
and the materials selection just right. In that period, we also fabricated all the cast
glass, which was very time-consuming. Each piece was in a kiln for three days
and there were thousands of these pieces, so, we had six or seven kilns going over
a period of two and a half years. Imagine the commitment of the client. You don't
have a site and you're making the cast glass!

**You mention site, because now that you see it in situ, you think, it has to be up
there on its own overlooking the city and seen from afar. Was that a difficult
process?**
Finding the right site was one of the most difficult processes. We went through
five sites before we found this one. There is this other aspect, which is much
more difficult to speak to — this project felt like it had a helping hand all the way
through. It wasn't going to just let you do whatever you wanted.

It had its own mind.
It had its own mind, its own agenda. It wasn't going to sit just anywhere; it had to
have the right site. And it couldn't be built any old way.
    I know that the higher our aim, the more challenging our task. There were
forces at work, all along the way, guiding us.
    I would be remiss if I did not praise the House of Justice for guiding this project
every step of the way and if I did not acknowledge a greater hand, which we all feel
has in every way steered us through this process.

So, how did the site finally appear?
That was one of the magic moments of this project. One of the sites offered to us

by the Government was in what they call the Twin Hills; it's the Central Park of Santiago. It took a year of conversation and an act of Parliament for this project to receive 17 or 18 hectares of land on the mountain. We thought this project would become iconic for the country. But, when it was accepted, various religions started to oppose it, and it became a hot bed of debate in the newspapers.

It became divisive.
Yes, and the House of Justice thought, "Well, that goes against the purpose."

So the decision was to withdraw, and we asked to search for another site. By then, the project had won nationwide attention. In fact, somebody was with me in a taxi, and said, "Do you know who this is?" Just as a joke. "This is the architect of the Bahá'í Temple." The taxi driver turned around and said, "So, where is it going to go?"

At that time, we were working with the Canadian Government, as well as the Ambassador and his group, and they asked if I could host a group of Chilean architects. I said we would be happy to. Two of them came up to me and said, "Really, you cannot go back out to our original site," which was about 40 kilometres outside of Santiago. "It's a beautiful area but no one will go." So, I said to one of them, Pablo Larrain, "How am I going to find a piece of land in Santiago? If this land is going to be found, it will come from a Chilean." He called me shortly thereafter with a tip. Pablo had found this land that belonged to a private school in Santiago. It took almost four years to negotiate the deal, but that's how it started.

One of the most mysterious moments of the project for me was when we were being shown the land and they took us to the pond. For some reason, I started to walk about half a kilometre. I walked to the place where the Temple now stands. We put a stake down in the very spot. I had felt the Temple there.

It was a memorable journey, led by Robert Cook, with Julian MacQueen and Douglas Henck, as well as Tiago Masrour and Adriana Balen. We had truly amazing project management by both Doron Meinhard and Justin Ford in our

Sketch by Siamak Hariri
of the Temple set against
the Andes.

Toronto office. In Chile, Claudio Orrego, currently the intendant of the Santiago Metropolitan Region, and Marisol Rojas, architect and consultant to the project, were invaluable to us.

All the energy of that Temple coalesced in that one place. You could feel why the arc of the mountain behind it works so beautifully with the whole city, like a tapestry, sitting there and the combination of the mountain and the city right at that elevation was absolutely perfect. From that point, we began our drawing of the site plan, and it has not moved from that spot.

Was landscaping integral to this project?
Yes. At the beginning we could not figure out how to have straight paths to this curved building, so we took the geometry of the building and just extended it out.

There is a journey between the street and the destination. It slows you down.
Exactly. Even the cars are held back. The buildings with amenities are buried into the hill. You have to go up a long stair to arrive at a terrace with the most extraordinary view of the city. We put this long and thin reflecting pool at the base, and then everything spins around. This is all a series of prayer gardens. The brilliant landscape architect Juan Grimm used indigenous plants with beautiful trees only found in that region. And Juan is a very special soul. He is not a Bahá'í, but he told me he had a strange dream about these curved paths, and that there were hairs in the water, with fish nibbling at the hairs.[4]

When a visitor comes up the hill to the building, do you have a hope for how they will respond? Do they become quiet? Introspective?
It should be a place where you feel connected to your inner self, as well as to the Divine. So this idea that it has an oculus that becomes an eye, through which the sun moves, and as a star pattern moves all day long and measures time and measures movement but is absolutely still, is a time honoured concept. It goes back to the most ancient philosophies of pantheistic thinking. But, we wanted it to be a universal place.

Once that visitor reaches the inside of this space, this volume, it has a certain warm, simple, austere feeling.
It's just wood floor and wood benches. No pulpit, and no clergy. The theory is that everyone should feel moved in this space of quiet reflection. Everybody's experience is their own. The architecture cannot be exclusive-feeling. It should be welcoming to all people of different strata.

It doesn't matter whether you're the poorest of the poor or the richest of the rich. It doesn't matter whether you're the most powerful or the least powerful. Here, everyone has a rightful place and a connection. It's a really interesting challenge architecturally — to make a space that is noble for everyone. You realize your own humanity and your own position within the scheme of things. You're not that important.

There's no test to pass, no confirmation hearing, to find out whether you're a member or not. There are no members here.
Everyone has this relationship with the Divine. It binds us all. The Temple should feel like that. This was an important design constraint — if it's too pretentious, or too referential to a single religion, iconography or form, it won't work. My hope is that a child of fourteen will want to go there. Not so easy. Or someone who absolutely has no faith will feel comfortable going there. It is meant to bridge all of that, and say, "This is everyone's Temple."

I think I would be happiest if people feel like this is their Temple. Someone from Paraguay or Uruguay or Bolivia could come and say, "That's my Temple," and have a connection to it.

What has been the reaction from the broader Chilean community to the project?
Very positive. It's captured a lot of their imaginations. You know, we wanted the Bahá'ís to love it and feel like its speaking up rather than down to their own hopes and dreams. But also, this has to be an important project for South America. We want people to really feel like it is their Temple.

In a way, the Bahá'í Faith is putting forth an alternate way of thinking about spirituality that is not based on traditional structures and rules and so forth. It's very new — the person with the Divine. It doesn't seem to be mediated, like so many other things.
In the Bahá'í Faith the notion of mediation is no longer necessary; everyone can investigate faith themselves now. Everyone has responsibility. You can't say, "Well, that's what my rabbi or my clergy told me to do and that's why I did it." No, the onus is on you; there's nothing between you and your relationship to God. That's new.

I think that's core. This structure is universally available to people from every possible background, but, at the same time, it's one on one.
It's one on one even though it's a singular space. There are all kinds of alcoves, where people can be in their own space within this space. In that sense, you have unity, but you also have diversity. The same goes for the pattern of the geometry on the outside — you can't take a single piece out, but yet, every piece is different.

It really stopped being architecture when they raised the Bahá'í symbol, which is called "the greatest name." It stopped being the Temple that was architecture, and became something else.

What does it say?
"O Thou Glory of the Most Glorious." Simple in location, centred in the oculus, it belongs in the middle, and is the only piece of iconography.

In your practice, is this the outlier of the kind of structures you've been building your whole career?

It needed to be special. You feel the DNA of the practice in the detail, the materials, and the sensibility, but the form needed to be special.

You also have your museums, and knowing the difference between the two is very important. Maybe some of the more institutional projects can be part of this group, too, since they help define a civilization.

They do need to be special. If you go back to Angkor Wat, Greece, Egypt, China, and South Asia, the built forms survive, as well as the iconography carved into these buildings. It's one of the most telling and durable expressions of any culture.

I agree.

How will this experience influence future projects? Will it shape your approach to work you would normally be doing in a city like Toronto?

I think so. How could it not?

1 Bahá'u'lláh, "Glory of God" (1817–1892), was the founder of the Bahá'í Faith.
2 "Whensoever the light of Manifestation of the King of Oneness settleth upon the throne of the heart and soul, His shining becometh visible in every limb and member. At that time the mystery of the famed tradition gleameth out of the darkness: "A servant is drawn unto Me in prayer until I answer him; and when I have answered him, I become the ear wherewith he heareth..." For thus the Master of the house hath appeared within His home, and all the pillars of the dwelling are ashine with His light." – Bahá'u'lláh, *The Seven Valleys*.
3 'Abdu'l-Bahá (1844–1921) was the eldest son of Bahá'u'lláh.
4 There is a well-known story in the Bahá'í Faith that recounts a dream Bahá'u'lláh's father, Vazír, had about his son: "Bahá'u'lláh appeared to him swimming in a vast, limitless ocean. His body shone upon the waters with a radiance that illumined the sea. Around His head, which could distinctly be seen above the waters, there radiated, in all directions, His long, jet-black locks, floating in great profusion above the waves. As he dreamed, a multitude of fishes gathered round Him, each holding fast to the extremity of one hair. Fascinated by the effulgence of His face, they followed Him in whatever direction He swam. Great as was their number, and however firmly they clung to His locks, not one single hair seemed to have been detached from His head, nor did the least injury affect His person. Free and unrestrained, He moved above the waters and they all followed Him." – *The Dawn-Breakers: Nabíl's Narrative of the Early Days of the Bahá'í Revelation*.

INTERLUDE LIGHT

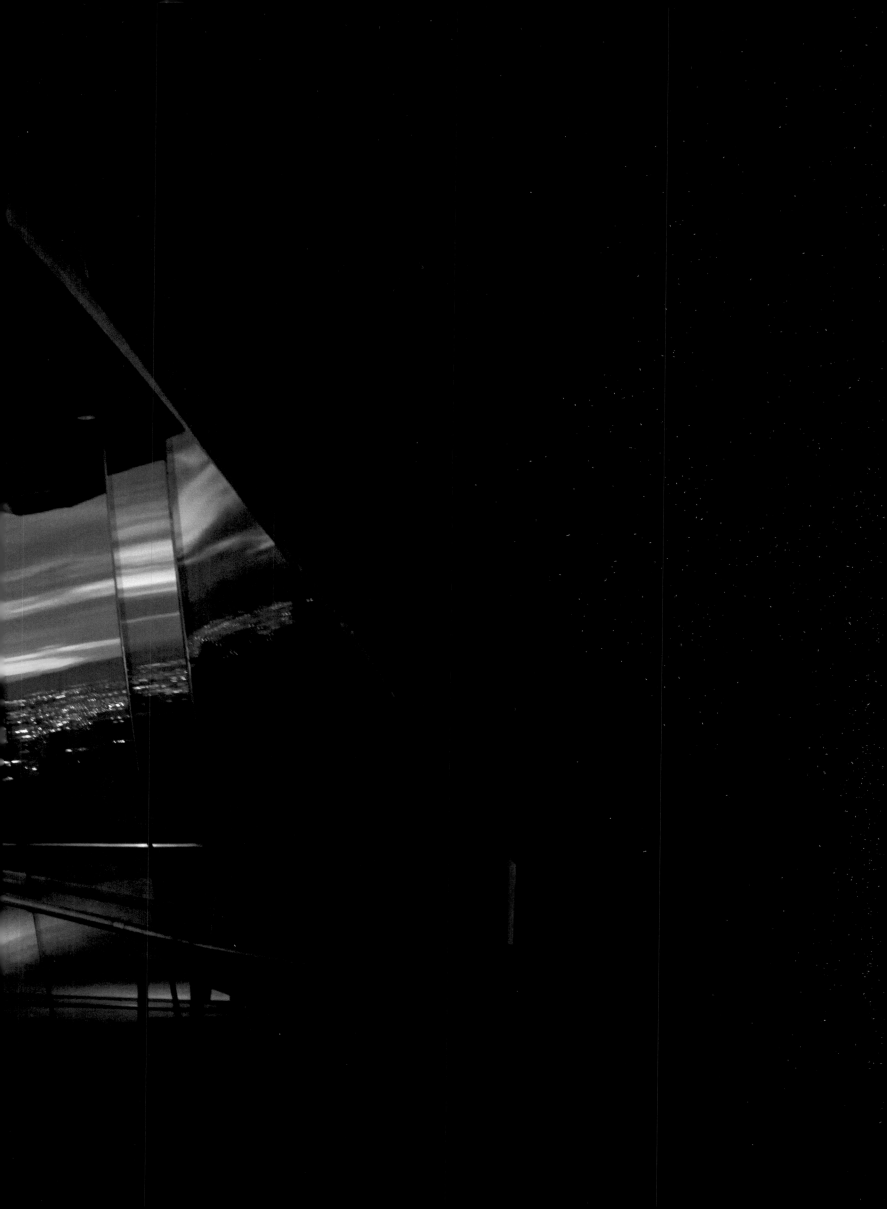

CONCEPT In 2003 the Bahá'í international community embarked on a journey to realize the eighth and final continental Temple in Santiago, Chile.

The design brief was deceptively simple: a nine-sided, one-room structure welcoming people from all sides. The architectural challenge was considerably more complex: to create a sacred structure for prayer, designed to serve the needs of humanity, bringing together science and religion, worship and service, and antiquity and timelessness with modernity. The Temple needed to express the fundamental Bahá'í concept of the oneness of spiritual truth, the oneness of religion, and the oneness of humanity. Absent of clergy, pulpits, and iconography, the space would invite worship without intermediaries or idols. A new expression of worship looking for a new expression in form.

The catalyzing inspiration for the project was found in the Bahá'í writings: if God decides to answer your prayer, you become infused with His light. The team became immersed in the exploration of creating a building that would go beyond simply allowing light in, towards the possibility of creating a structure that would capture and become alive with a spiritual, embodied light.

To achieve this aspiration, the team was inspired by experiential phenomena: the magic of dappled sunshine beneath a canopy of trees; the swirling skirt of a Sufi dancer; and the abstract, yet powerfully structured paintings of Mark Tobey. The interplay of seeming contradictions — stillness and movement, simplicity and complexity, intimacy and monumentality — culminated in a solid structure capable of dissolving in light.

Hand sketches and physical model making were paired with burgeoning digital design techniques and technologies, including 3-D printing and Maya modelling software, to explore and articulate new forms and complexities, allowing the team to illustrate their intentions. Although it took 14 years to complete, the final structure of the Temple remains remarkably true to these early sketches.

The Temple set against the sculptural backdrop of the Andes.

An international call for submissions by the National Spiritual Assembly
of the Bahá´is of Chile for the *Mashriqu'l-Adhkár* of South America
resulted in 180 entries from around the world. Hariri Pontarini
Architects was one of the four shortlisted firms. The office embarked on
a four-month design exploration combining traditional physical models
and hand sketches with the latest digital fabrication and modelling
techniques. The abundant variety of studies that resulted, paired with
inspirational images, is displayed linearly in the photo collage above.

Demonstration Chair by Gebrüder Thonet; Japanese woven basket; *Lovers of Light* by Mark Tobey.

Sufi whirling; Renaissance painting of robes: *Saint John the Baptist*, by Francesco Del Cossa, c. 1473, Pinacoteca di Brera; fractured resin pattern.

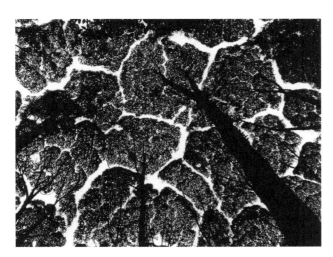 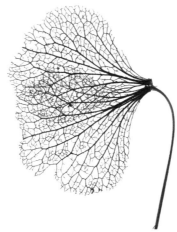

Dappled light through a canopy of trees; photograph of the skeleton of a *Hydrangea* petal by Peter Nijenhuis.

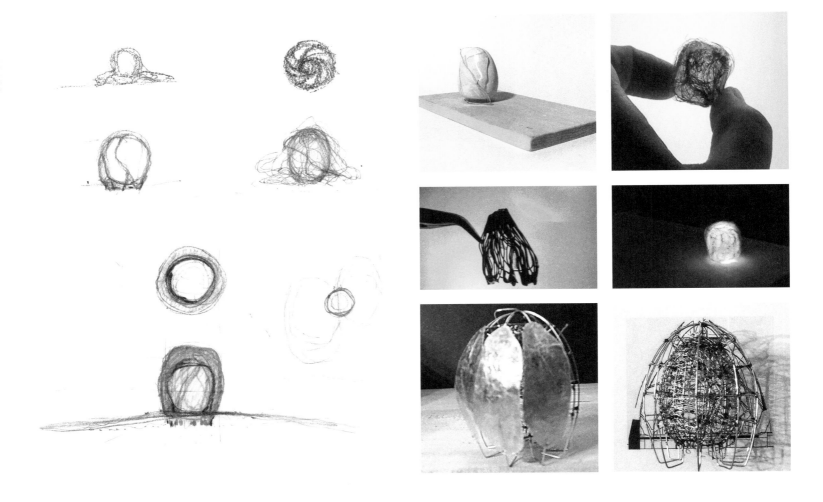

Early design iterations were grounded in the overarching concept of light, but also attempted to convey traits discovered in inspirational objects and images: stillness and movement, a simple line creating a complex totality, the soft draping of fabrics and cloths, and structure within abstraction.

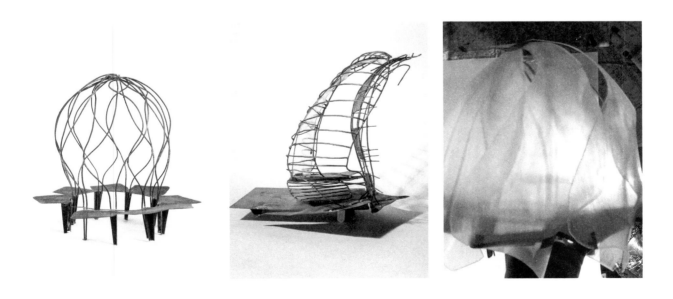

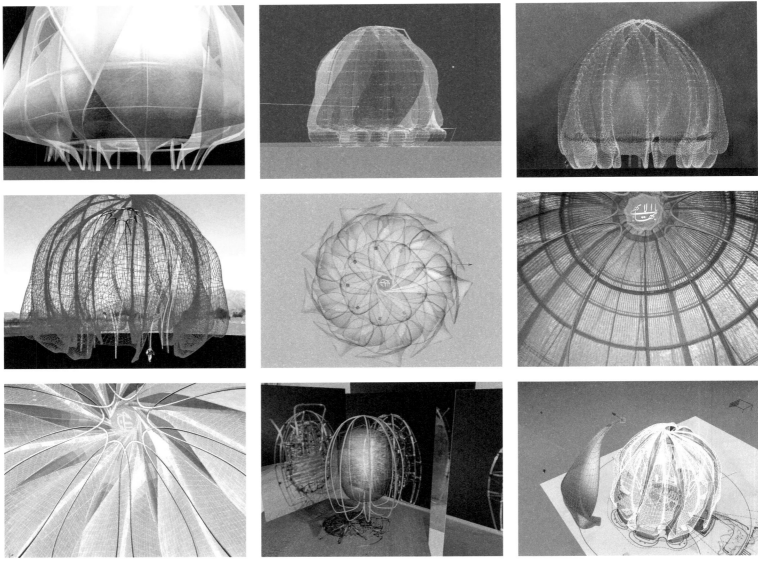

Screenshots from Maya model development.

Emphasis was given to proliferating ideas by not staying statically bound to a sole medium of representation, thus digital modelling studies ran parallel with physical modelling and drawing. The use of Maya software, originally designed for the film and entertainment industry, broke from the more traditional use of CAD (computer aided design) software. Maya produces objects using a series of surfaces rather than solids, giving the designer an ability to finely adjust the shades of transparency and light, as well as freely sculpt and manipulate complex shapes.

Building the structural form model (left); expressing the sculptural form of a single wing as a negative space (right).

Stills from the fly-through prepared for the competition submission.

Longitudinal site section, competition phase.

The design exploration culminated in a Maya model that sculpturally represented the desired aspirations: nine identically torqued wings that, when combined, speak of motion and asymmetry along with perfection, with delicate curves and a transparency that would capture the light passing through.

Through a digital fabrication technique, then in its infancy, called rapid prototyping, and now commonly known as 3-D printing, a physical representation of the Maya model was produced. This 1:50 scale model, lit from within, was the culmination of the competition submission.

Completed Maya model for competition phase.

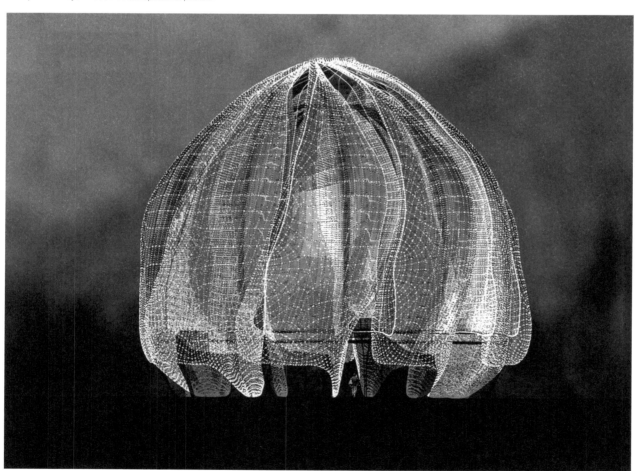

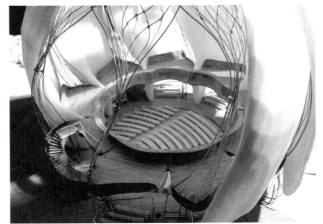

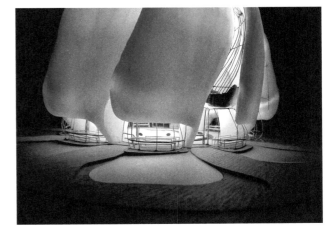

Completed rapid prototype model for competition phase.

Rendering of Temple at dusk.

PLACE In an authoritative Bahá'í statement by Shoghi Effendi, indication was made that the Mother Temple of South America be erected in Santiago, Chile. In 1967, in anticipation of construction, the Bahá'í community acquired a piece of land in the northeast portion of the city, which, at the time, was still rural.

In the 40 years between the initial land acquisition and the start of the project, the area surrounding the site became developed economically in a manner that left it unsuitable for a Bahá'í House of Worship. Thus, after the competition was complete and the project awarded, the design team began a search for a new location. This search extended over three years and resulted in the discovery of the current site at the foothills of the Andes, in the commune of Peñalolén.

The site is exquisitely located between the sculptural backdrop of the Andes to the east, powerful in its raw majesty, and a panoramic vista that takes in all of urban Santiago to the west. Being slightly removed from the metropolis, the fresh air and silence bring a sense of serenity to the visitor, while still allowing for a visual connection to the city.

The master plan consists of an axial stair and a curving accessible path that connects the various edifices and supporting elements on the 9.3-hectare site. Along with the Temple, there are a series of ancillary buildings that are buried in the hillside and covered with planted roofs, parking, and a variety of outdoor gathering spaces.

The Temple's geometries spiral out towards the nine surrounding reflecting pools and further to a series of meandering paths within a 7.8-hectare garden. The earth has been carefully sculpted to create playful vistas, enhance the sense of procession, while gracefully intertwining path, garden, water, and edifice.

The garden concept by landscape architect Juan Grimm similarly conceives of the planting as emanating from the Temple, with vibrant flowers and flora embracing the building and transitioning outwards, seamlessly blending into the indigenous context of the site.

The Temple at dusk.

1. The Linderos Site.

2. Scouting the site at Lo Curro.

3. Surveying Colina site on horseback.

4. Metropolitan Park.

5. Siamak Hariri at the chosen site in Peñalolén.

After the original site, purchased in 1967, was deemed unsuitable for the development of the Temple, the team was assigned the considerable task of finding a replacement. This intensive search saw the team journey through four distinct locations throughout Santiago and its surrounds, and included a site in Metropolitan Park, located at the centre and most visible location within the city. Meeting with local politicians and stakeholders, the team struggled to find a suitable home for the anticipated building.

Map of Santiago showing
the five explored sites for
the Temple.

1. Linderos
2. Lo Curro
3. Colina
4. Metropolitan Park
5. Peñalolén

The search for a site concluded in Peñalolén, a commune to the east of
central Santiago that is situated on the foothills of the Andes, almost
1,000 metres above sea level. The 9.3-hectare site provides two stunning
and opposing canvases as backdrops. Looking west, a panoramic view of
urban Santiago laid out like a carpet, a sparkling dense image of one of the
largest metropolitan areas in South America. Looking east, untouched
nature, the sculptural form of the Andes, rising quickly from the site to peak
at 6,570 metres above sea level.

The Temple under construction, as seen from Metropolitan Santiago.

Bordering the urban and natural: the context plan locates the Temple site between the city of Santiago and the Andes mountain range.

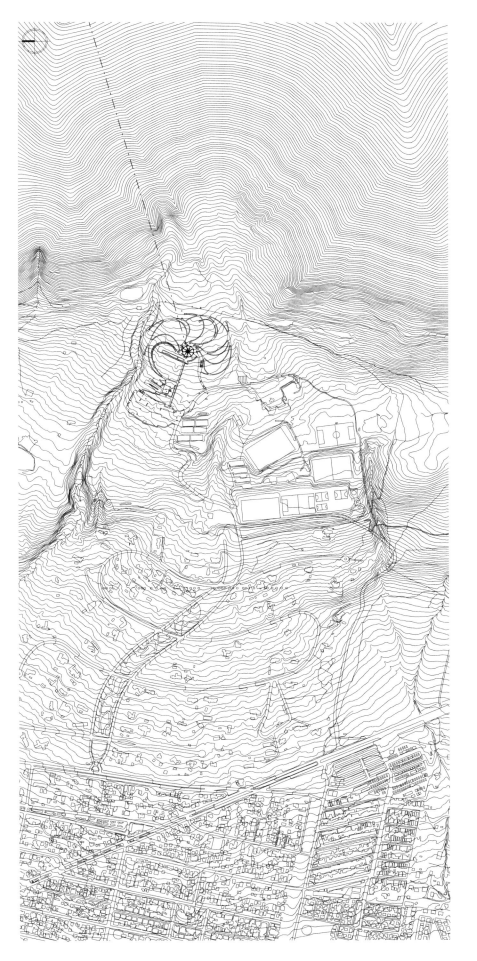

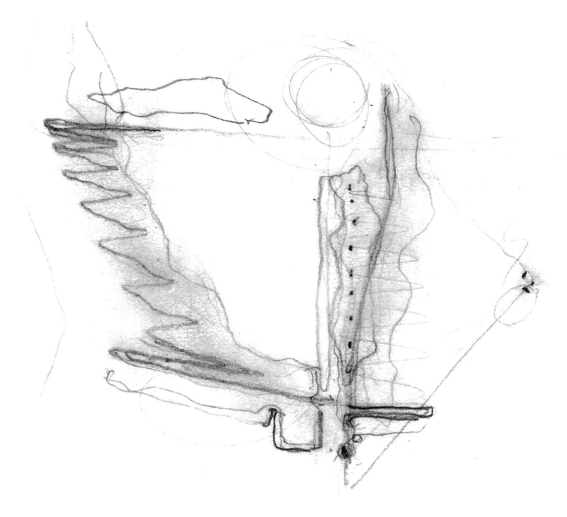

Sketch (above) and model (below) studying relationships of landscape, path, and building.

The site where the Temple rests is 500 metres long in one direction rising towards the Andes, and between 150 and 300 metres wide in the other. The design requirements were not only for the Temple itself, but for a generous garden, ancillary buildings including a reception building, centralized restroom facilities, various security and maintenance structures, as well as parking for the visitors. The site, large in comparison to the building program, required that the relationships and distances between the structures and programs be studied carefully. A central idea emerged; one of procession. A more functional zone was delineated, one that would be left behind by the guests, who then walk a substantial distance, granting the time to spiritually prepare themselves before entering the sacred space of the Temple and gardens.

Early site model studying grading, earth movement, and relationships between elements.

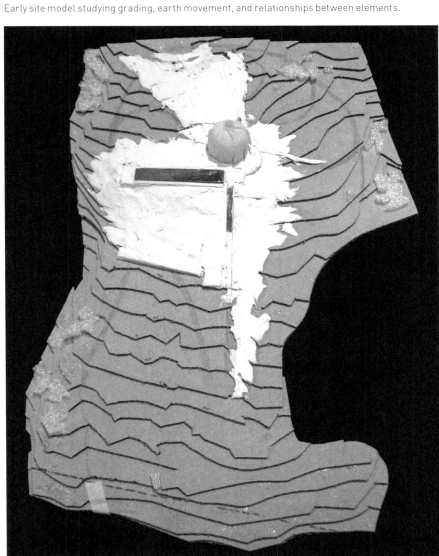

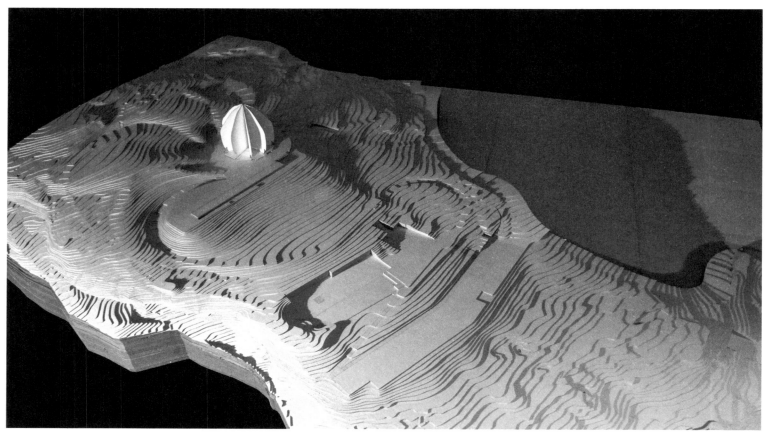

Detailed site grading model, studying the carving of the curving paths in the landscape and their relationship to the Temple podium development.

Study model of reception building with green roof, buried in the slope of the hill.

Considerable sculpting and forming became fundamentally important due to the steady incline of the site and the requirement for a flat area of gathering around the Temple. Substantial earth manipulation was also required to integrate an access route, to lead less mobile visitors up the steep slope from the parking and ancillary buildings to the Temple. Additionally, the decision was made to bury the ancillary buildings in the slope of the hill, leaving only one of each of their elevations fully exposed. This worked two-fold, allowing the roof of these buildings to be planted, leaving the view towards the city from the Temple unobstructed, and to keep the interiors cool in the hot summer months.

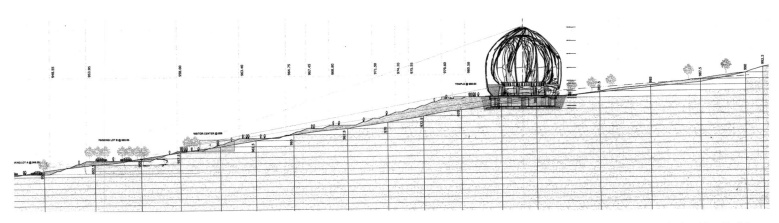

Site section study showing cut and fill of earth movements, site lines from the Temple, and vertical relationship of buildings.

In the Bahá'í Faith the garden is held to equal importance as the Houses of Worship themselves. Where traditionally the structure of these gardens have been strictly formal, the design team's decision instead was to take cues from the curves of the Temple, allowing these curves to emanate outwards and inform the paths that would form the framework of the garden. These meandering paths laid out the basis for the water pieces, earthworks, and planting that followed.

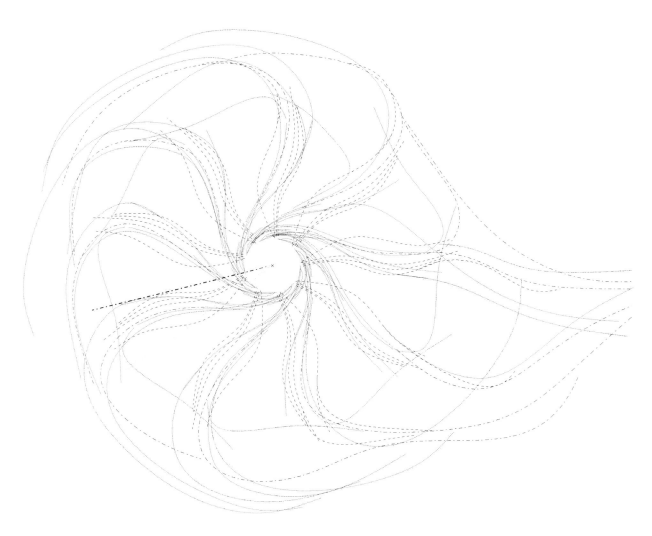

Early digital sketch depicting the concept of radiating paths.

Landscape sketch by Juan Grimm.

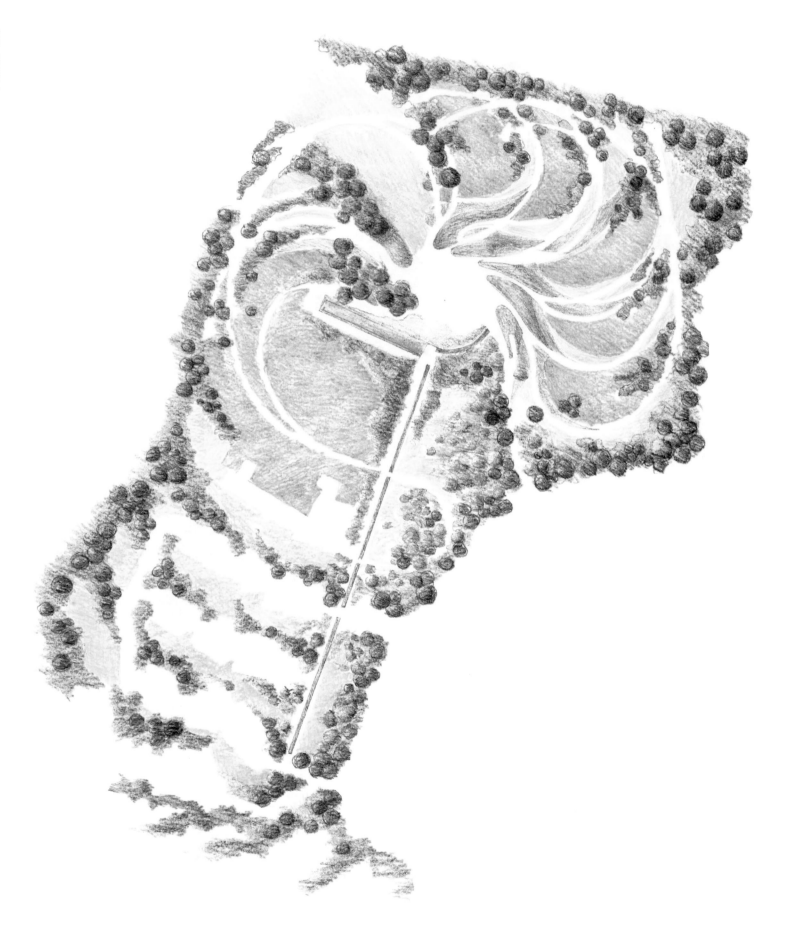

Early rendering of the planting plan by Juan Grimm.

Working with Chilean landscape architect Juan Grimm, the Temple was conceptualized as a drop of water on a relatively arid site. The Temple and its nine water features provide symbolic hydration to the lush and sculpted land masses that are designed to appear as if they are reaching towards the source. As the landscape radiates outwards from the Temple, it seamlessly blends into the context of the site with a slow gradation towards naturally occurring greenery.

Tree species used in the
landscape design.

1. Espino
   Acacia caven
2. Jacaranda
   Jacaranda mimosifolia
3. Magnolio de Flor
   Magnolio sulangeana
4. Manzano de Flor
   Malus floribunda
5. Peumo
   Cryptocarya alba
6. Quillay
   Quillaja saponaria quillay
7. Molle
   Schinus latifolius
8. Roble americano
   Quercus falcata
9. Pimiento
   Schinus molle

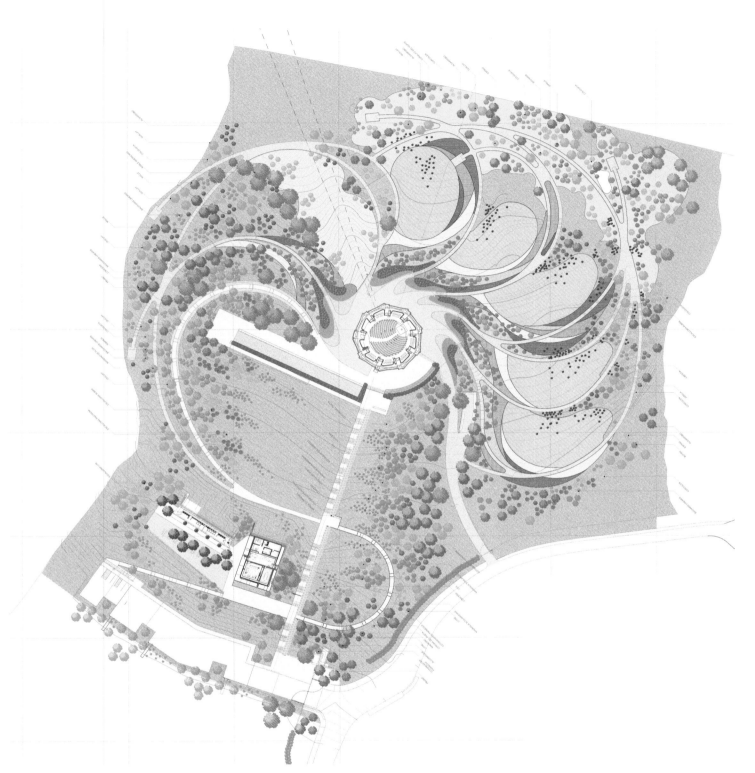

Planting plan by Juan Grimm.

INTERLUDE LANDSCAPE

TECHNOLOGIES Realizing the complex curves conveyed in the conceptual design required the studio to look beyond traditional three-dimensional visualization software typically used by the architectural industry, towards modelling platforms geared to fabrication and manufacturing. A technological leap was required to translate the initial design model into a robust, information-rich, detailed model that could then be used, in lieu of traditional construction drawings, to fully describe the intricacies of the Temple for construction and fabrication. Dassault's CAD/CAM CATIA software, used primarily by the automotive, aviation, and aerospace industries, was selected for its ability to gracefully manage the large amount of geometric and informational data required for such a complex and irregular form, and to transfer this information directly to fabrication machines.

The CATIA model evolved into a complete source of geometry and information. Combining structural, mechanical, electrical, and cladding information within a single architecturally managed master model enabled the team to ensure this complex interplay of elements was consistently aligned with the overall architectural vision.

This technological investment, at the early design development stage, also facilitated an architecturally led exploration into advanced fabrication techniques that could achieve the complexity of form. These studies culminated in a full 1:6 scale prototype model of the steel space-frame structure. It was from this scale model that many of the fabrication techniques were first developed and tested.

The final fabrication of the steel superstructure was made possible only through advanced fabrication techniques, from CNC plasma cutting to 5-axis CNC milling machines. This included: the boundary members, large structural steel tubes tied to the concrete base through embedments and coming together in a hollow steel ring at the oculus; connection nodes locking the elements of the structural space frame together; and gussets allowing secondary elements to connect to the boundary members. In Germany the multitude of parts were assembled into manageable sections, meticulously labelled, shipped, and assembled on site.

The wings of the Temple, soaring above the mezzanine — a space for quiet contemplation.

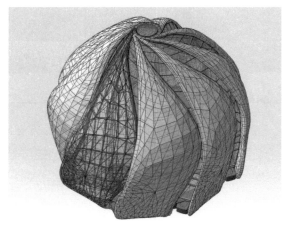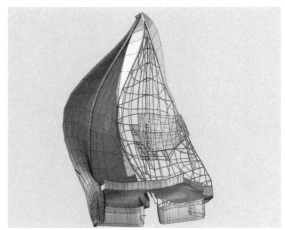
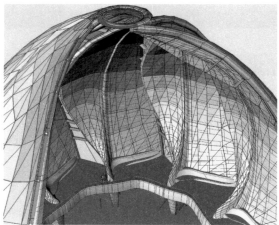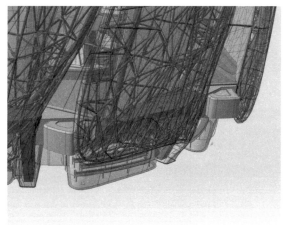

Screenshots from the CATIA model development.

The benefits of implementing such a malleable software as Maya in the competition phase of the project, quickly became problematic when attempting to solidify the free form design into reality. It was immediately evident that carrying the ambitious conceptual design forward would require a leap both in 3-D modelling software capabilities, and the role that these technologies would take in the projects development.

Dessault System's CATIA, an integrated management software intended to facilitate industrial design processes from concept to manufacturing, used heavily in the aerospace, automotive, and aviation industries, was chosen to further the development. The architecturally built and managed CATIA model became the comprehensive central source of geometric information for the remainder of the project. Here all elements would first be "built virtually" and tested to ensure spatial and aesthetic conformance to the architectural vision.

Screenshots from the CATIA model development.

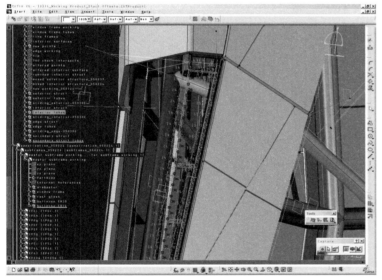

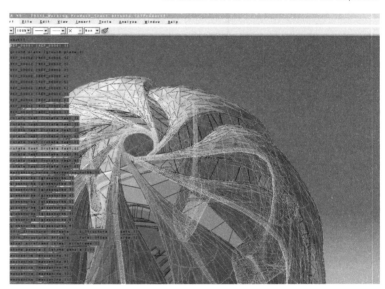

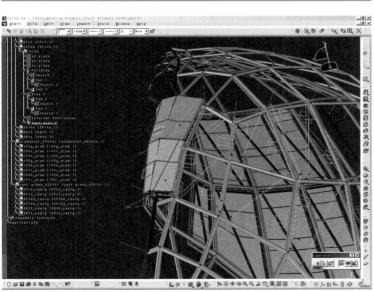

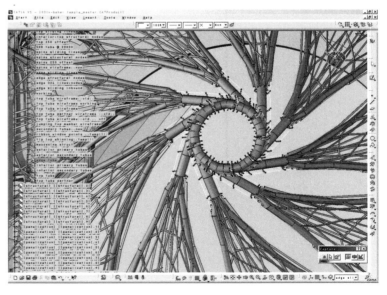

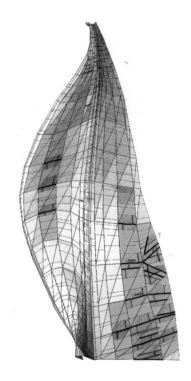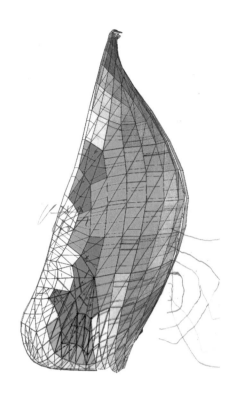

One of the first developments towards constructability was the division of
each wing, originally sculpted in Maya, into panels that could be effectively
and efficiently fabricated. This study ran in parallel with material and
cladding detail developments, and integrated restrictions such as the cost
of creating curved panels vs. flat panels, maximum yields of raw materials,
and engineering concerns, to arrive at a jointing pattern. Aesthetically the
final jointing pattern was designed to achieve a proportional harmony at
various scales, and convey a sense of movement and rhythm in tune with the
overall design.

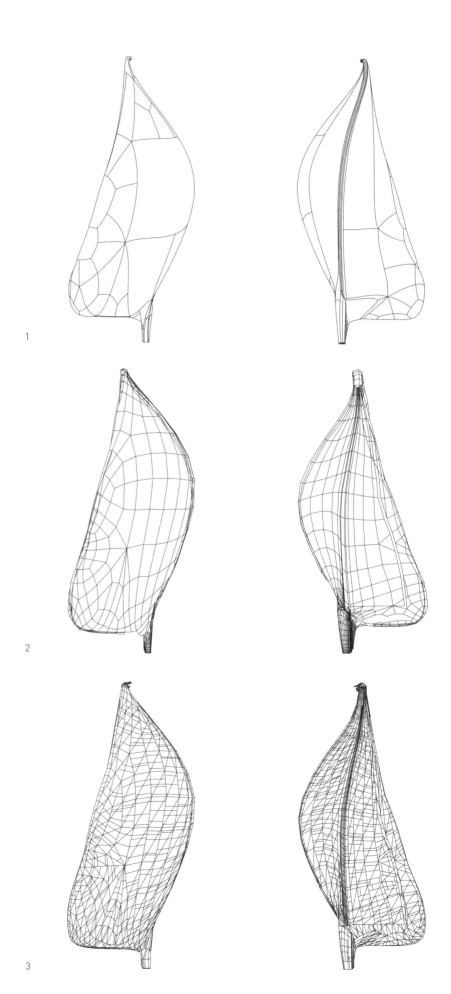

Progression of
panel jointing.

1. Jointing inherent in the
Maya NURBS model.

2. Basic tessellation into
quadrilaterals. These
facets first emerged in
the rapid-prototyped
model.

3. Triangulation to
create flat paneling and
further breakdown of
jointing with material
considerations.

Building the 1:6 scale model of the steel space-frame structure.

Diagram showing how the digital model was used to build the 1:6 scale model: first the wing frame was rotated, then the nodal points were projected down to a ground plane. This indicated the locations and heights for individual steel pipes. The steel pipes were placed in the appropriate coordinates, then nodes were placed on top and connected.

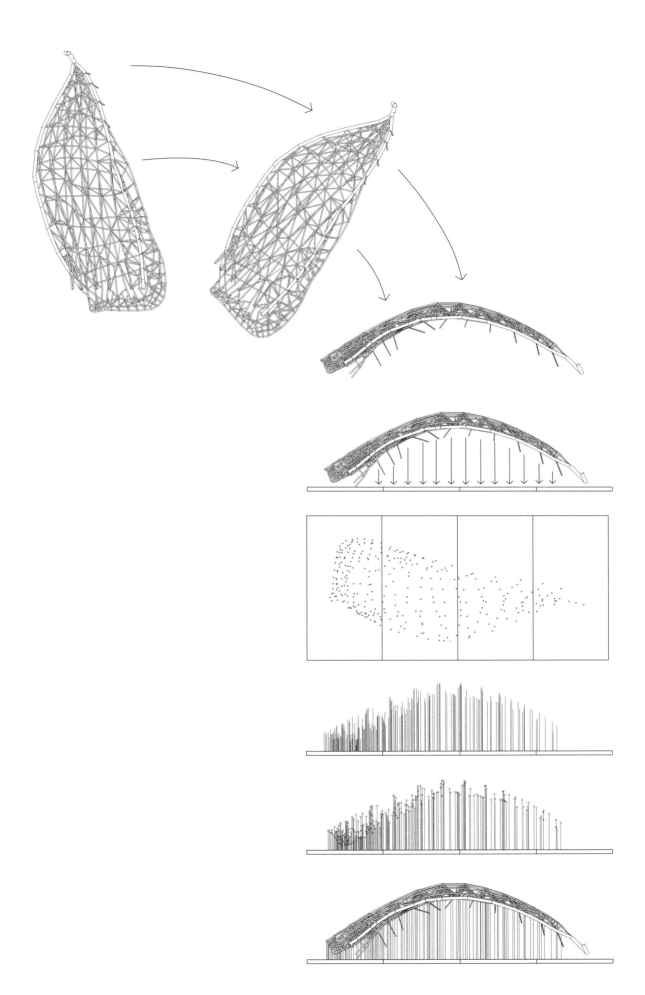

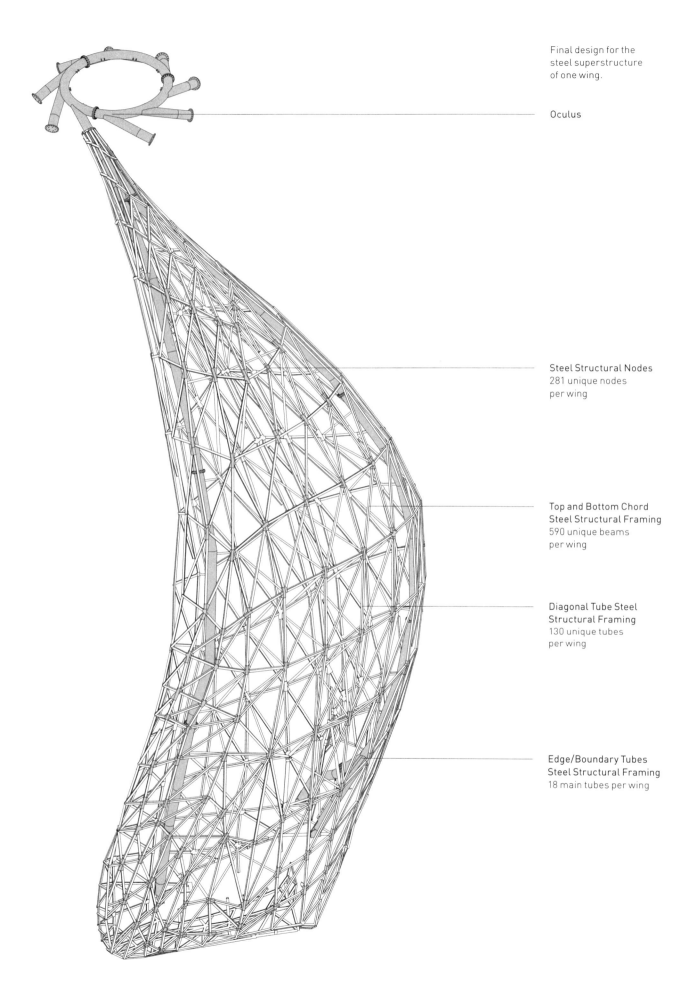

Final design for the
steel superstructure
of one wing.

Oculus

Steel Structural Nodes
281 unique nodes
per wing

Top and Bottom Chord
Steel Structural Framing
590 unique beams
per wing

Diagonal Tube Steel
Structural Framing
130 unique tubes
per wing

Edge/Boundary Tubes
Steel Structural Framing
18 main tubes per wing

Development of the structure continued in parallel with material developments. Both physical and computer modelling analysis was conducted by cladding and structural engineers for strength, thermal stress, seismic, and wind performance. The structural performance in a seismic event was of specific interest due to the long history of strong earthquakes in Chile.

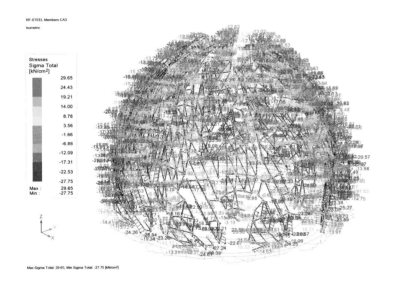

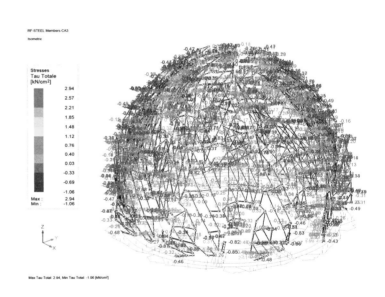

Computer model analysis of seismic forces, and their effects to the proposed Temple structure.

Oculus steel ring structure on fabrication jig.

In 2012 Gartner Steel and Glass from Germany was awarded the contract to fabricate the main structural steel and cladding systems for the Temple. The team worked in close collaboration with Gartner's engineers and designers to optimize the design. Final fabrication of the structural steel commenced the following year. Thousands of individual steel components were fabricated in various locations throughout Germany using state-of-the-art digital fabrication techniques. These parts were then assembled into manageable pieces, meticulously labelled, and shipped to Santiago for installation.

Detail of oculus steel ring structure on fabrication jig (above). Boundary structural members laid out in full using a CNC cut jig. The process is almost identical to the 1:6 scale mock-up produced in the design development stage (below).

Cut gussets allow a simplified connection of secondary elements to the main structure.

Close-up of CNC-produced template for boundary member fabrication. Specific data required for identification is directly engraved onto the template.

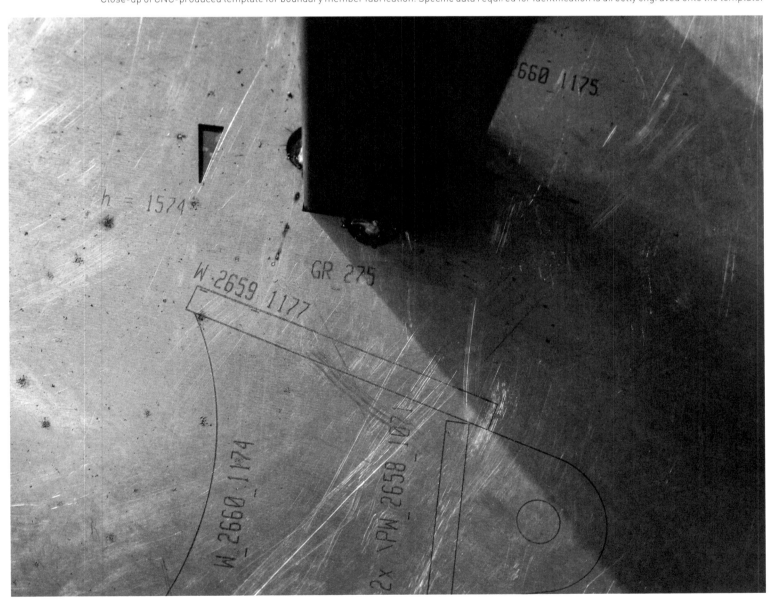

CNC plasma cutting of the rough node shapes in solid steel; a 5-axis CNC machine takes the rough-cut nodes, carves and machines them.

In order to minimize the physical space taken by the nodes within the wing structure, each nodal face is CNC-milled to form an exact geometrical offset to the cladding elements they hold. They must also accept and negotiate square and round structural tubes that arrive at a multitude of unique angles. This precision and complexity is evident in the 281 unique nodes per wing.

The completed nodes are bundled on pallets for shipping.

INTERLUDE INTERIOR

MATERIALS The vision for the Temple began with the concept of light — to design a building that would not only let light through, but also allow the light to be captured, refined, and cast, as if radiating from within.

An intensive investigation resulted in the development of two fully realized cladding materials: an exterior layer consisting of cast-glass panels developed solely for the project, and an interior layer composed of an exceptionally translucent marble. Between dawn and dusk these materials become infused with the wide range of seasonal colours that dance across Santiago's sky; the light that is filtered to the inside of the building shifts from white to silver to ochre, then blue to purple. At night, the materials allow for an inversion of light, whereby the Temple, lit from within, casts a soft glow against the Andean mountain range that borders the city.

Research and development of the exterior cast-glass cladding took four years of experimentation in collaboration with Toronto-based glass artisan Jeff Goodman. The translucent marble panels that form the interior walls of the Temple were chosen from a quarry in Portugal for both clarity and the delicate quality of the veining. Each wing of the nine-sided Temple contains over 1,120 unique pieces of cast glass and over 870 unique pieces of translucent marble. Final assembly for both cast glass and marble elements took place in Germany before the completed pieces were shipped to Santiago.

Hand-finished interior materials such as walnut and leather were selected to bring a warm textural quality. Patinaed bronze for elements such as doors, exterior soffits, and railings was chosen as a durable complement to the interior cladding materials. Together, this palette of materials helps to create a sensuous experience, merging the touch of the artisan with the precision of the digital machine.

Interior marble during construction. The wing to the right has yet to receive cast-glass cladding on the exterior.

Early glass-casting experiment in sand.

To achieve a new sense of transparency, one that would manifest the concept of embodied light, but at the same time be durable enough for exterior use, the team underwent the ambitious task of developing a new material. In addition to characteristics of translucency, the ability was paramount to convey the timeless qualities of ancient materials that would weather beautifully with age. The idea was born to combine the transparency of glass with the monolithic qualities of stone. Toronto-based glass artisan Jeff Goodman, known for his beautifully finished decorative glass works, was engaged to collaborate on the endeavor. This creative collaboration into the visual possibilities of glass casting yielded a stunning array of variations in method, texture, and tone.

Early cast-glass prototypes.

Fabrication of flat cast-glass sheets for the exterior cladding.

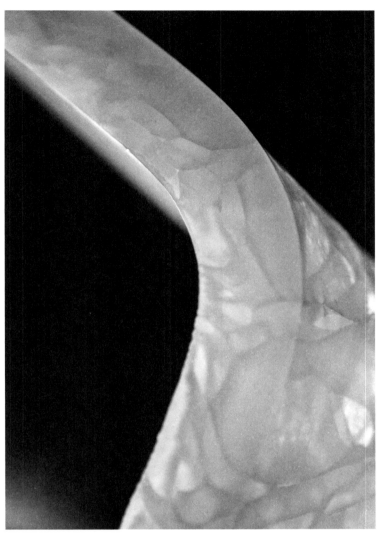

Detail of curved cast-glass pieces.

The result of four years of research and development was a matte-textured cast glass, 32 mm in thickness, that would both diffract and diffuse the passing light. The material is made with two diameters of borosilicate glass rods, which after being carefully broken into strata, are placed and fired in custom-sized and programmed kilns. The material, when lit, comes alive with subtle variations of translucency, movement, and colour.

A percentage of the cladding, both for the interior stone and exterior cast glass, was conceived of as curved. Curved panels occur where the wing geometries curve too greatly to allow for flat, facetted panels. A process was developed to achieve these curved shapes in cast glass. Coined as 'slumping', foam moulds were first CNC-carved and concrete poured or shot onto them to produce a second mould. A flat cast-glass panel was then water jet-cut to shape and set atop the concrete mould, to then be put back into the kiln. During re-heating, the flat shape would 'slump' atop of the concrete mould and produce the desired curved shape.

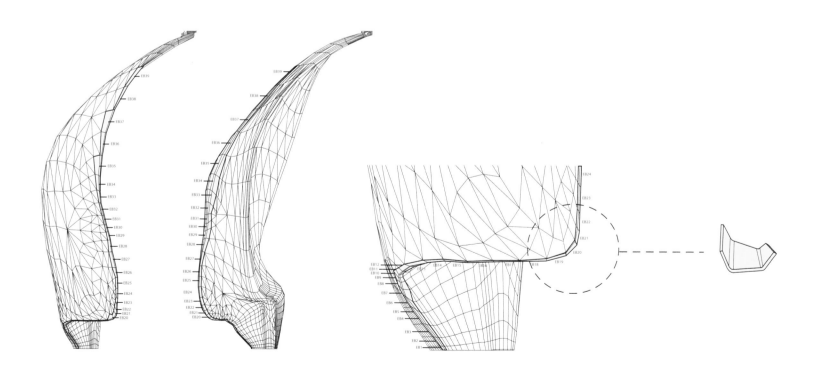

Process of 'slumping' cast glass into curved shapes.

Early slumped glass test at Jeff Goodman's Studio.

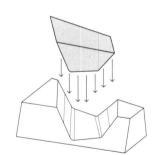 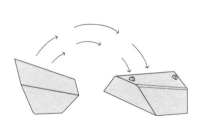 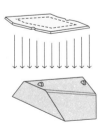 

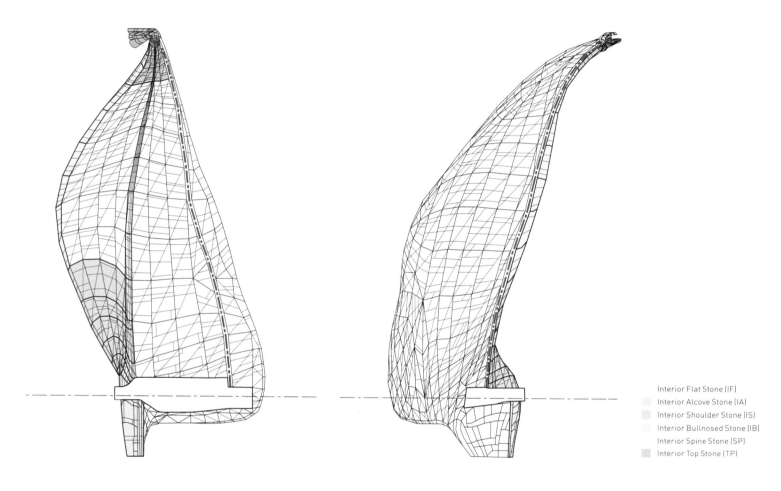

Interior Flat Stone (IF)
Interior Alcove Stone (IA)
Interior Shoulder Stone (IS)
Interior Bullnosed Stone (IB)
Interior Spine Stone (SP)
Interior Top Stone (TP)

Classification of various cladding components that make up the interior cladding of one wing.

An integral part of the development of the design was to classify the vast quantity of unique panels, both on the interior and exterior faces, into areas with distinct nomenclature. This allowed individual panels to be more easily referenced and developed depending on their distinguishing characteristics, challenges, and complexities. Playful names such as 'Shoulder Glass' and 'Spine Stone' were carried through from design to construction stages.

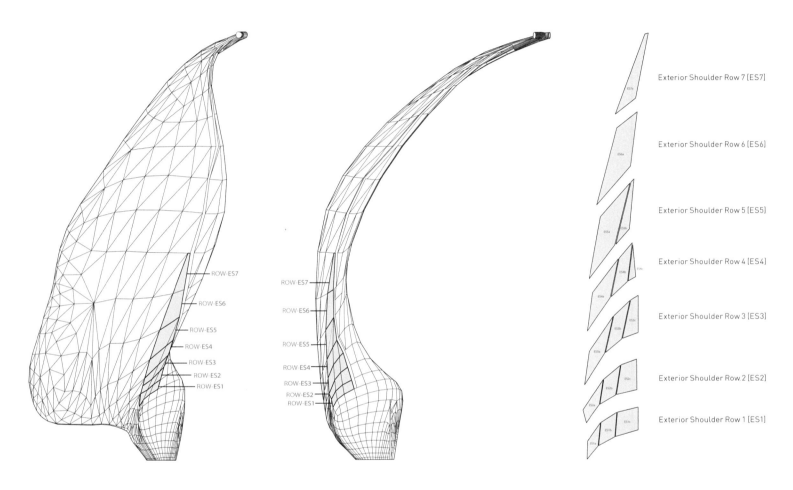

Breakdown of the panels that make up the 'Exterior Shoulder Stone.'

ROW-ES7

ROW-ES6

ROW-ES5

ROW-ES4

ROW-ES3

ROW-ES2

ROW-ES1

Exterior Shoulder Row 7 [ES7]

Exterior Shoulder Row 6 [ES6]

Exterior Shoulder Row 5 [ES5]

Exterior Shoulder Row 4 [ES4]

Exterior Shoulder Row 3 [ES3]

Exterior Shoulder Row 2 [ES2]

Exterior Shoulder Row 1 [ES1]

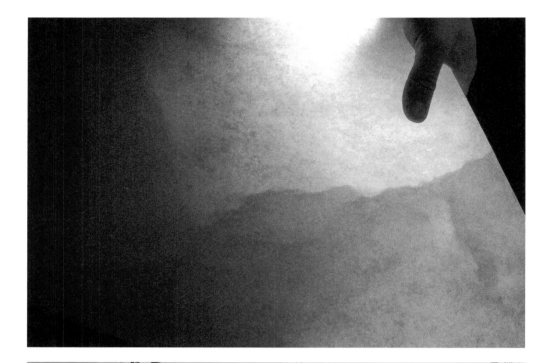

Light through a CNC-carved alabaster piece (top); test wall of cast glass variations (bottom).

Alabaster was originally selected as the primary cladding material for the Temple. However, after many rounds of vigorous testing the material was eventually deemed unsuitable for its fragility. The team uncovered that the elegant transparency of the material came largely from its composition, which included substantial hydrogen content; hydrogen that would migrate from the material if its temperature rose above 35 degrees Celsius, leaving the stone not only brittle, but opaque.

Rather than resort to a costly mechanical system solely for cooling this delicate material, a replacement range of stone was investigated. Eventually a translucent marble, culled from a specific quarry strata in Portugal, was chosen both for its clarity and the delicate quality of its veining.

Visual mock-up of alabaster (top). Visual mock-up of Portuguese marble (bottom).

CNC-cutting of stone piece from a block; hand finishing of marble pieces using curved templates; finished marble pieces.

The marble cladding was fabricated in Portugal by French company EDM, near the quarry of its origin. As with the cast glass, a certain portion of this interior cladding needed to be made of curved panels. The stone was cut into a rough-sized block and then milled by a series of CNC machines, each machine refining the surface further. The final finish of the pieces was completed by hand, where custom templates were used to ensure a perfectly smooth transition between neighbouring pieces.

Details of CNC-carved stone pieces before hand finishing.

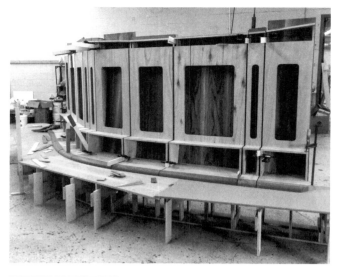

CNC-cut wood benches and finishes.

Bronze and wood elements were chosen to complement the principle cladding of cast glass and marble. Fabricated in Ohio from American Walnut, the wooden mezzanine and benches were corn-blasted to raise the grain and lend a weathered texture. Detailed 3-D scans of the complex site conditions, already completed, were taken to ensure the wood elements were fabricated with a high level of precision.

The bronze doors, exterior soffits and canopies, as well as detailed trims and handrails were fabricated in Germany, including the enormous pivoting main entry door made of artisanal cast bronze. These elements were painstakingly patinaed by hand to produce a precise colouration, tone, and patterning.

Bronze smelter (top); hand finishing of cast-bronze door (bottom).

INTERLUDE DETAIL

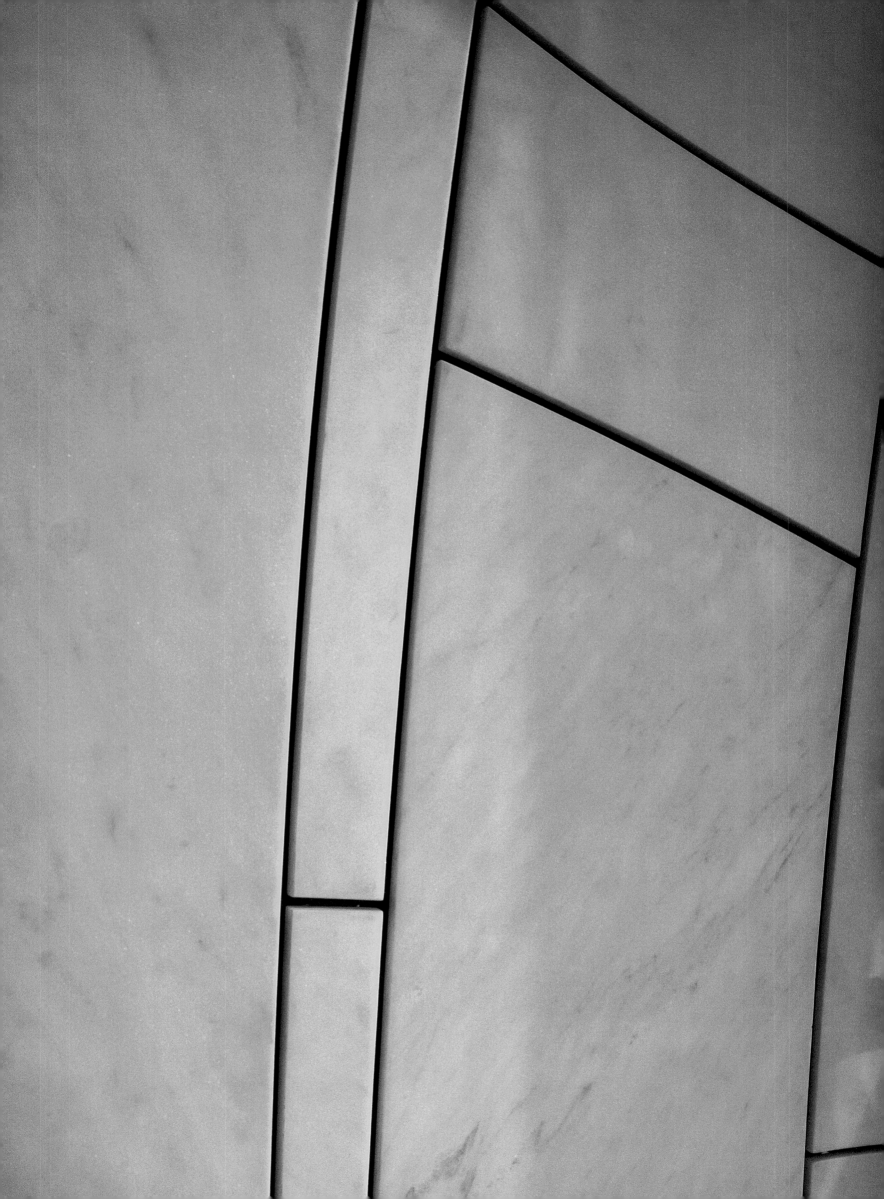

CONSTRUCTION The development of the site and excavations for the Bahá'í Temple of South America began in 2010. Two years later, the monumental task of constructing the Temple was underway.

Situated in an active seismic zone, Chile has long been prone to powerful seismic events. The Temple structure had to not only support the complex building, but also withstand these tremendous forces. A series of triple pendulum seismic isolators, placed on top of ten concrete columns rooted in the Temple's foundation, allows the building above grade to float, isolating it from any movement of the earth below.

After the concrete base was completed, installation began of the over 1,000 pre-fabricated pieces of steel, and assembled cladding panels of glass, marble, bronze, and wood, which continuously arrived in Santiago via shipping containers. Like a giant jigsaw puzzle, each meticulously labelled piece was installed in sequence, beginning with the steel structure.

Sitting atop the concrete mezzanine, a steel space frame delineates the interior and exterior faces. Made rigid by diagonal bracing members, the frame is shaped in accordance with the geometry of the cladding it supports.

The pre-assembled panels of marble on the interior and the cast glass on the exterior are both framed with aluminum and installed, using a toggle system, onto the structural space frame. The interior marble was installed first, allowing each piece to be positioned through the steel superstructure with the help of a tower crane. The exterior cast glass was then lifted into place.

Final interior finishing — curved balustrades and wooden benches; bronze framed glass alcoves; inlay detailing; canopies; and polished wood flooring — was carried out with craftsmanship and precision.

The construction and installation teams were globally diverse, spanning from Germany to Brazil, bringing their expertise in concert with the local Chilean workforce. Bahá'í volunteers from around the world also added their dedicated efforts to the construction of the Temple.

The custom-fabricated steel superstructure, assembled on site.

Aerial view of foundation, with rebar in process for ground slab beams (top); concrete foundation before backfilling (bottom).

Installation of a seismic isolator.

The cylindrical foundation, set six metres below grade, consists of ten reinforced concrete columns — one central and nine at the perimeter — tied together by steel bracing members. Installed above each of these columns are triple pendulum seismic isolation bearings which allow the remainder of the building from the ground slab upwards to be isolated from any seismic movements.

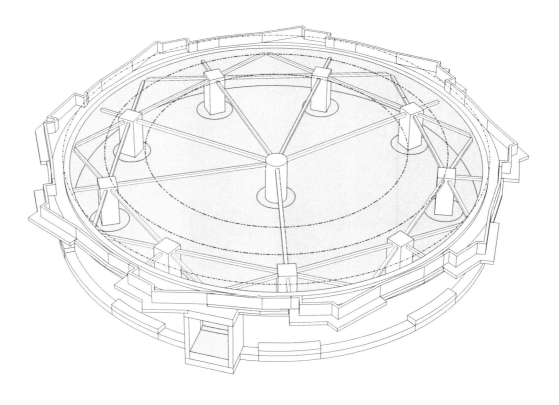

Axonometric drawing of concrete foundation.

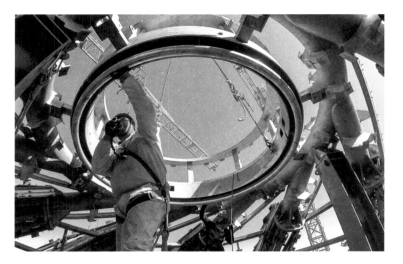

Oculus steel structure being lifted into place.

The concrete mezzanine slab, along with its nine supporting columns, were next to be poured. Steel plates that would eventually receive the steel superstructure were carefully placed and embedded in the concrete. A 30-metre high central scaffold tower was erected to precisely locate the steel oculus structure at the apex.

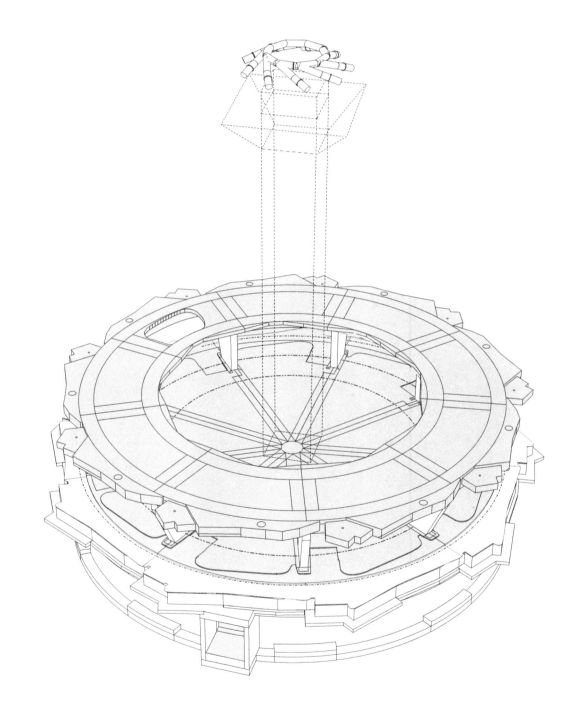

Axonometric drawing of concrete foundation and mezzanine with oculus steel structure installed on scaffold tower.

Boundary member being lifted into place.

Boundary members tied into oculus at apex.

Each of the nine wings is structurally defined by two large hollow steel
spines referred to as boundary members. These members meet at, and
are tied to, the oculus structure positioned at the apex. At their base,
the boundary members are anchored to steel brackets embedded in the
mezzanine floor slab.

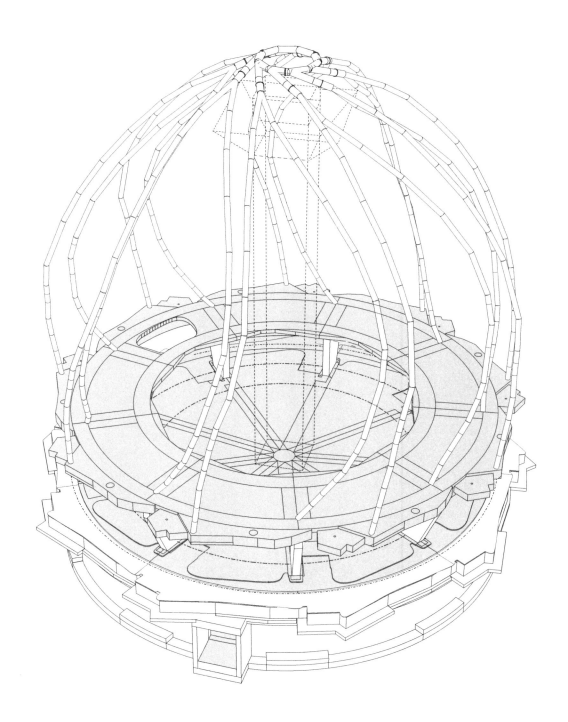

Axonometric drawing of concrete foundation and mezzanine with edge boundary steel members and oculus.

Aerial view of structural steel framing being completed.

Assembly of steel space frame.

The space-frame web of the steel structure is made up of custom-fabricated steel nodes, tubes, and sections spanning between the boundary members. In each wing, there are over 1,000 individual steel pieces, each with a unique length, requiring a unique nodal connection. This space frame directly follows the interior and exterior jointing pattern to ensure shadowing through the translucent materials is in harmony with the overall appearance of the Temple.

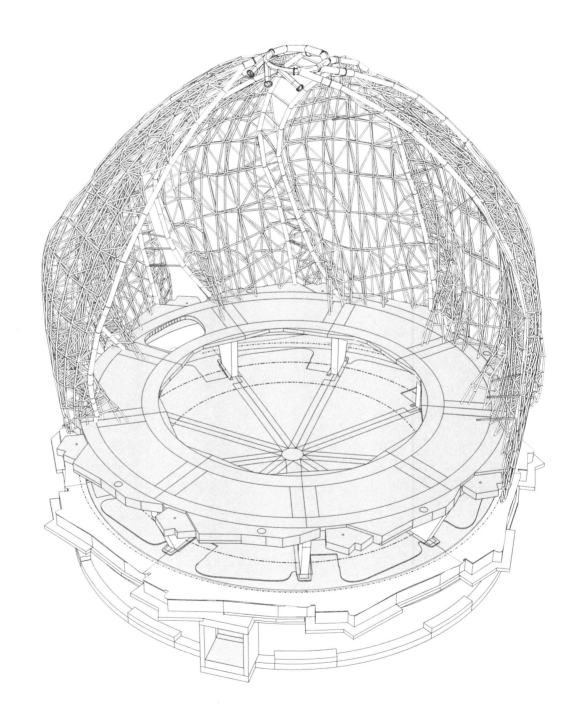

Axonometric drawing of completed steel structure on concrete foundation.

Installation progress of stone cladding panels.

Installing marble panels onto structural steel.

The interior marble cladding arrives on site assembled into panels containing multiple marble pieces installed on aluminum frames. These panels are lifted into place and installed onto the steel superstructure with a toggle system. The interior cladding is installed first so that it can be easily lifted through the steel superstructure.

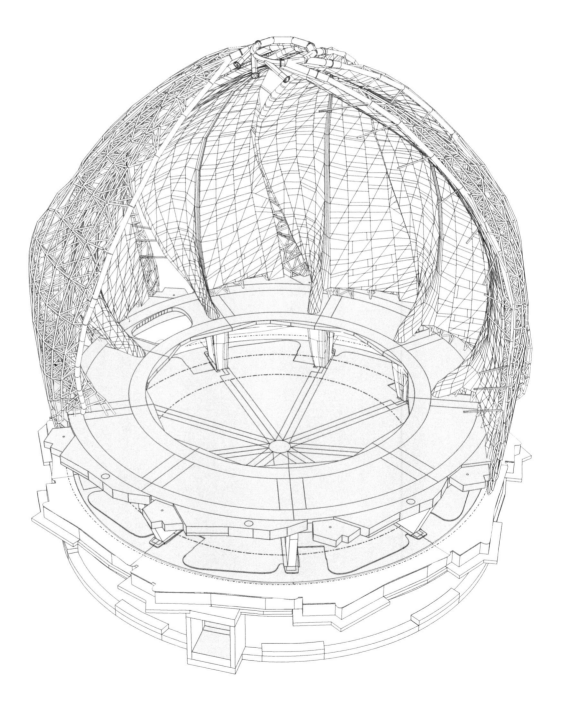

Axonometric drawing — cutaway of partially completed interior stone cladding.

View with partially installed exterior cladding.

Lift work installing cast-glass panels onto structural steel frame.

Similar to the interior cladding, the exterior cast-glass cladding arrives on site assembled onto aluminum frames. These frames are hoisted into place and installed with a toggle system onto the steel superstructure. Later the joints between panels are sealed with silicon.

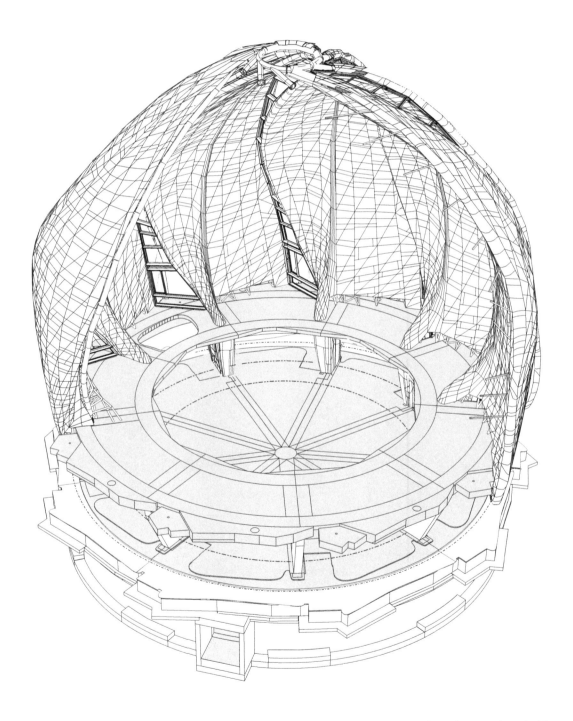

Axonometric drawing — cutaway of completed interior stone and exterior cast-glass cladding.

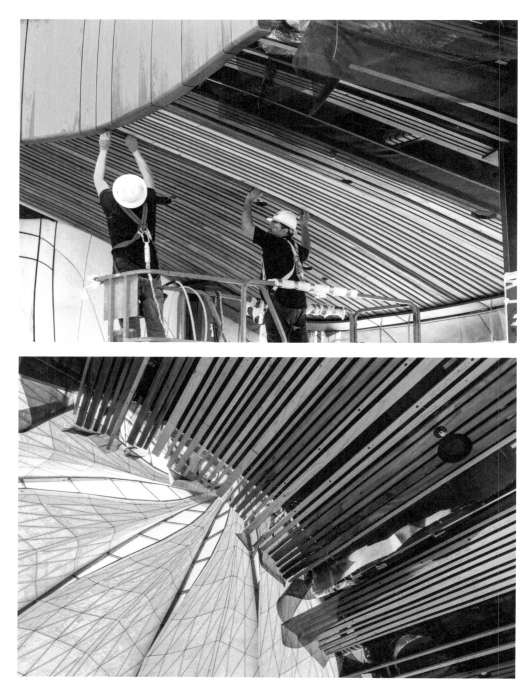

Installation of wood mezzanine soffit slats (top); partially completed wood mezzanine soffit (bottom).

The interior wood finishes of the Temple are made of American Walnut. The wood balustrade was CNC-cut and vacuum-formed in Ohio, then fitted and installed on site by means of steel supports attached to the concrete mezzanine. The wood slat soffit was installed as individual strips onto an aluminum rib system hung from the underside of the concrete mezzanine.

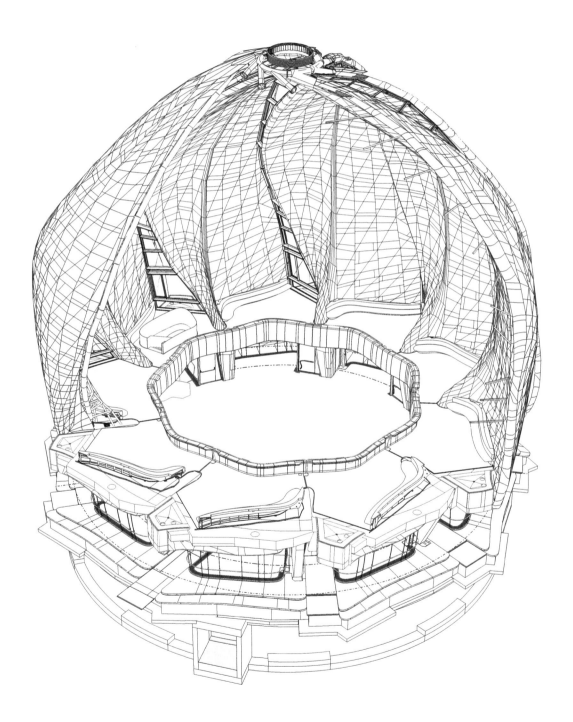

Axonometric drawing — cutaway of complete Temple.

INTERLUDE **WORKSITE**

COMPLETION The Bahá'í Temple of South America was presented to the public in October of 2016, the last of eight continental Temples. It was a journey spanning 14 years, resulting from countless hours of dedication from a global team which included hundreds of Bahá'í volunteers. This achievement was celebrated with a series of events and a three-day dedication ceremony in Santiago, Chile, attended by people from around the world and the international Bahá'í community.

Visited by tens of thousands in the first month after opening its doors to the public, it is as much for those of the Bahá'í Faith, as those of any other Faith, or no Faith at all. Without ritual, clergy, icons, or images, *Mashriqu'l-Adhkárs* are conceived to reflect an ideal of universal worship, for all to worship in their own way. Some sit and meditate, others are lost in quiet contemplation, some stare upwards in awe, and still others sing out in praise. The Temple comes alive with prayer.

Built to last 400 years, there is a hope that the Temple will continue to draw humanity closer to the Divine, to that quest for personal and collective perfection, betterment, refinement, reliance, and a longing for togetherness and unity. Stone, glass, wood, and steel become spiritual, and the measurable becomes immeasurable.

View from the mezzanine. The carpet was entrusted to the Temple by the Universal House of Justice.

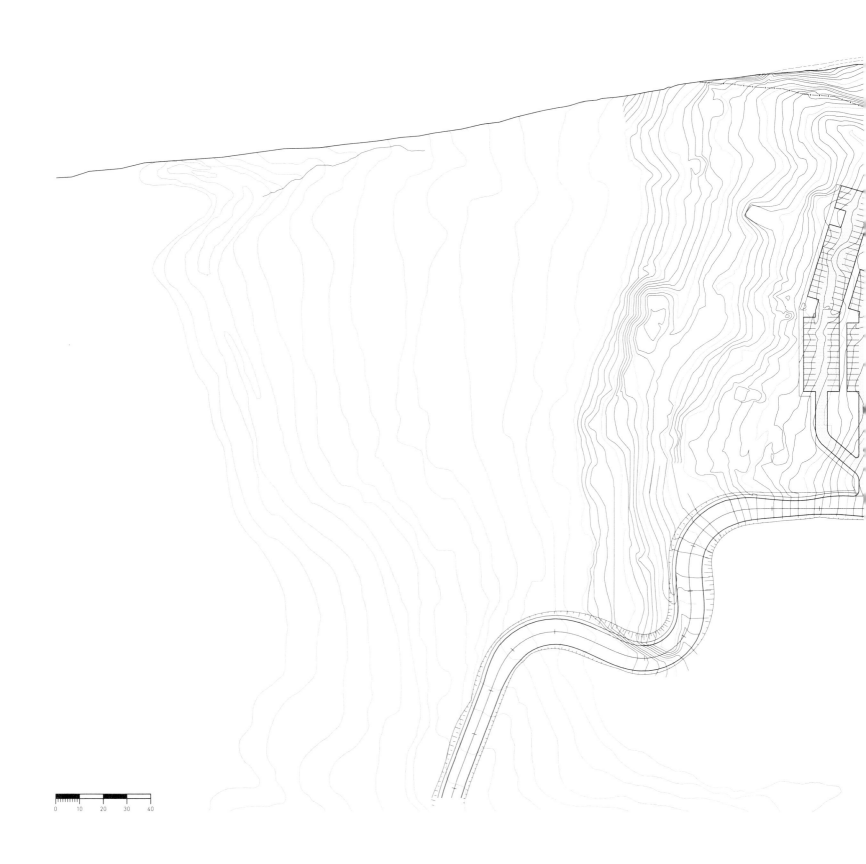

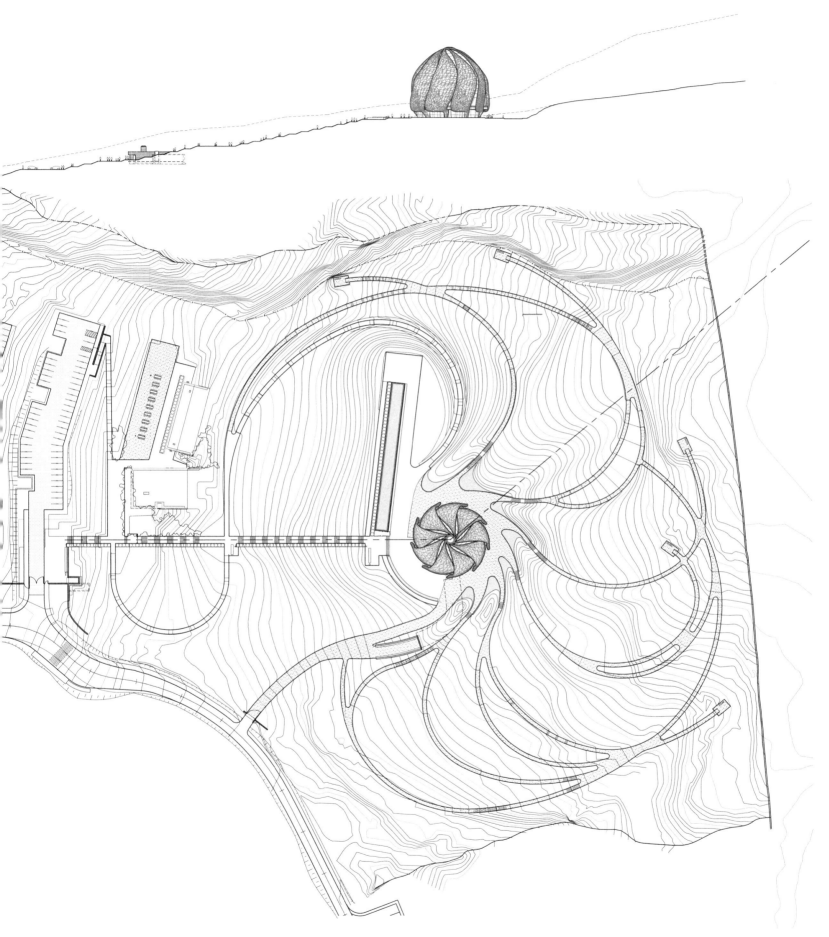

Site plan and section.

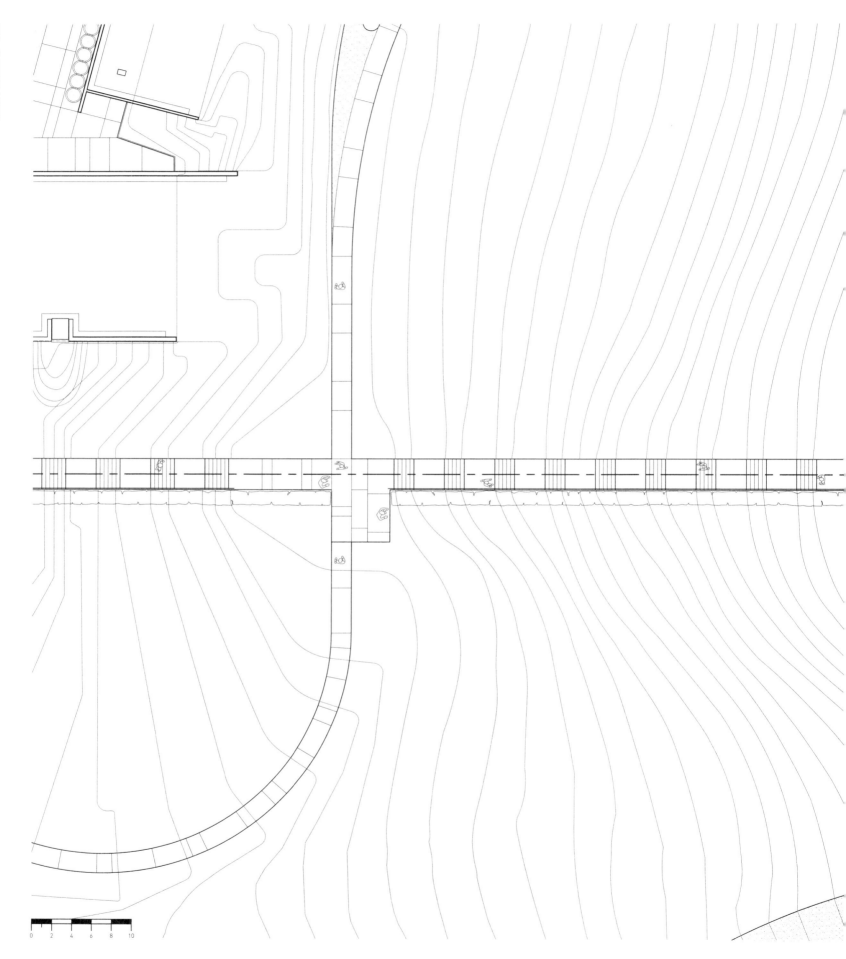

0 2 4 6 8 10

Site plan (detail).

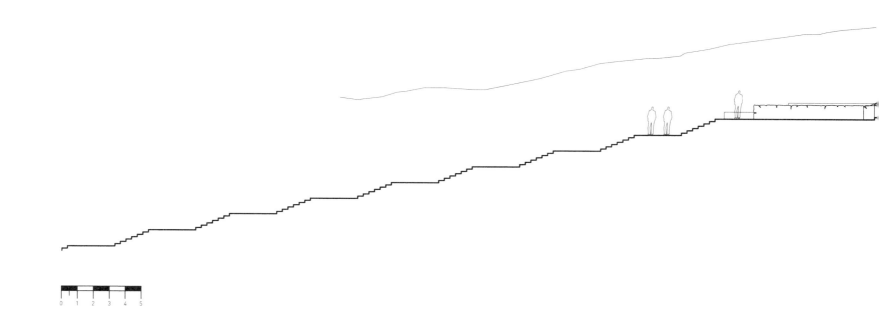

0 1 2 3 4 5

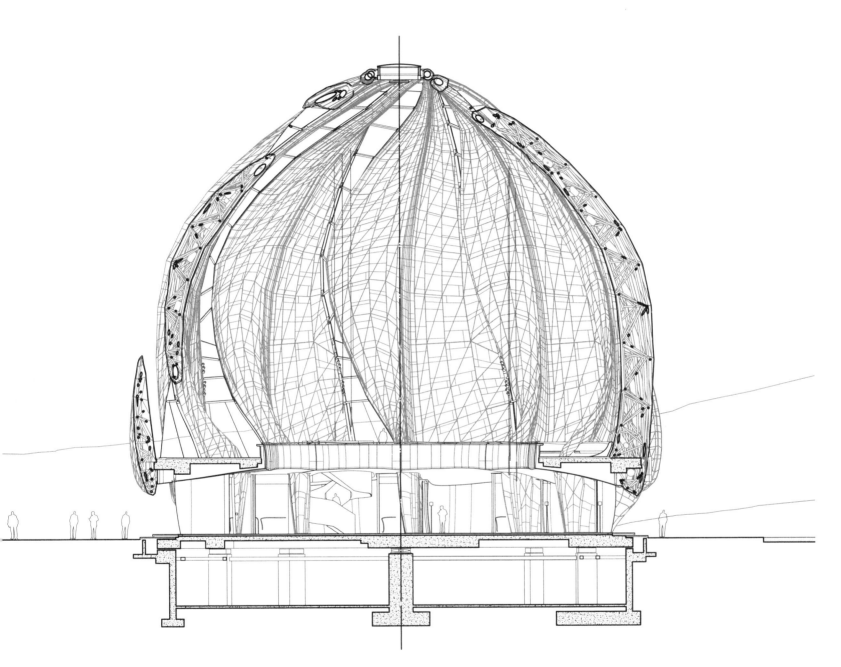

Building section.

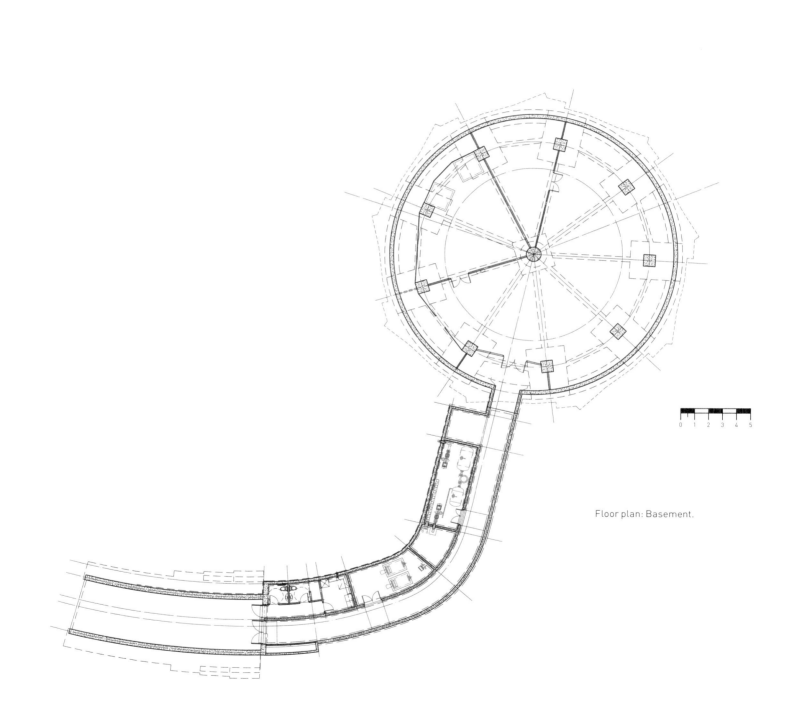

Floor plan: Basement.

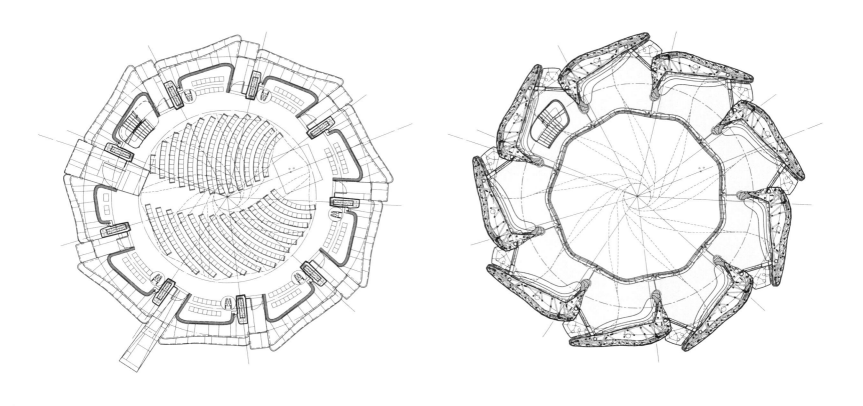

Floor plan: Ground.

Floor plan: Mezzanine.

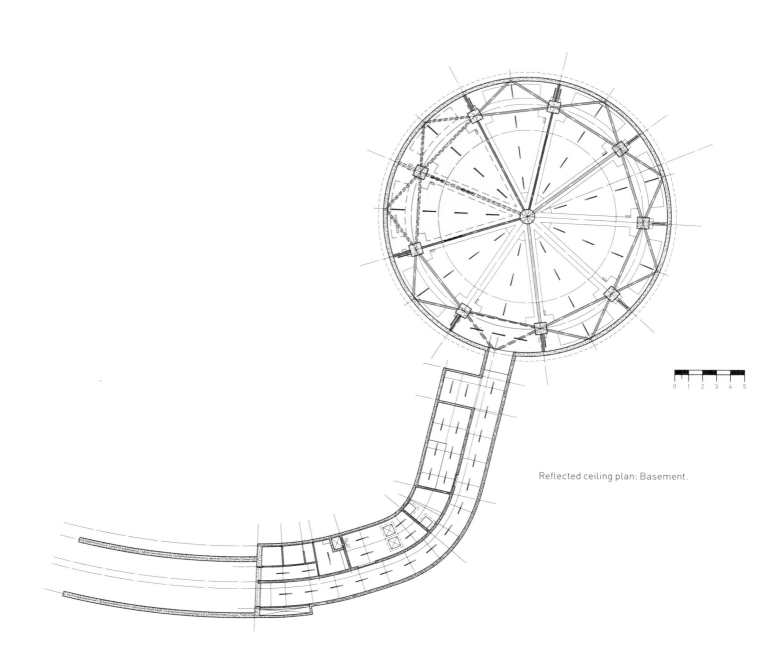

Reflected ceiling plan: Basement.

Reflected ceiling plan: Ground.

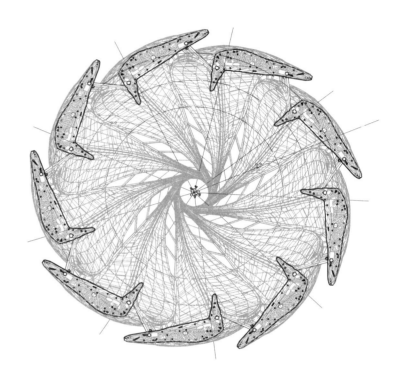

Reflected ceiling plan: Mezzanine.

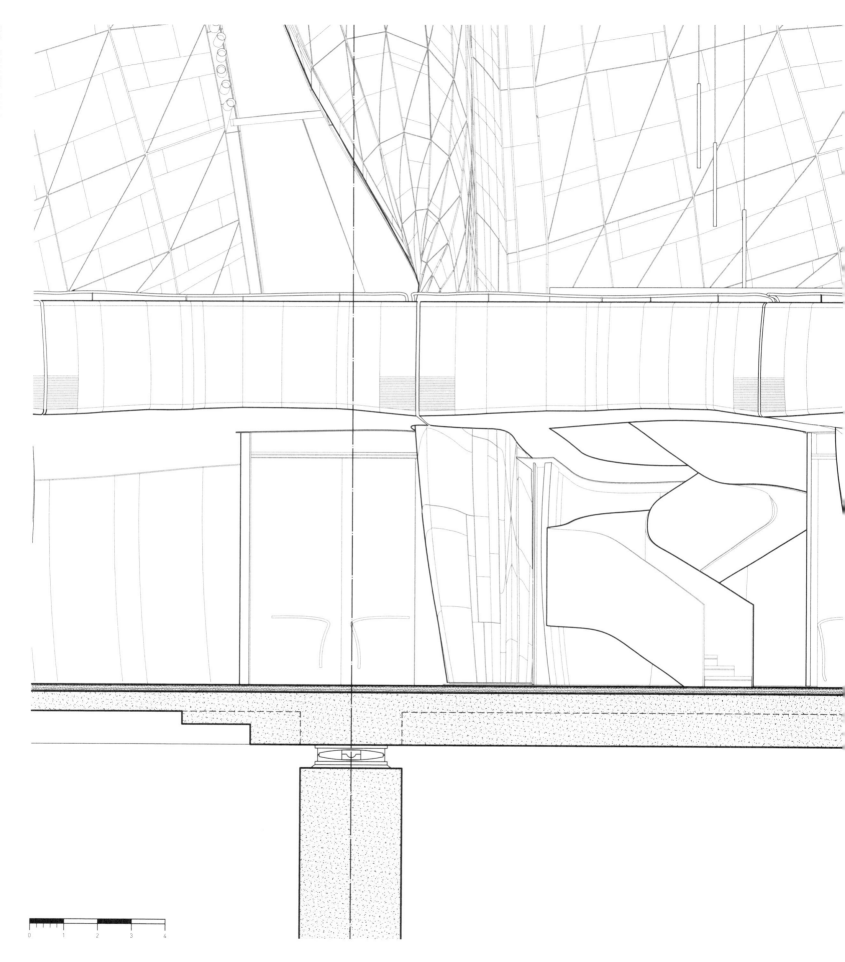

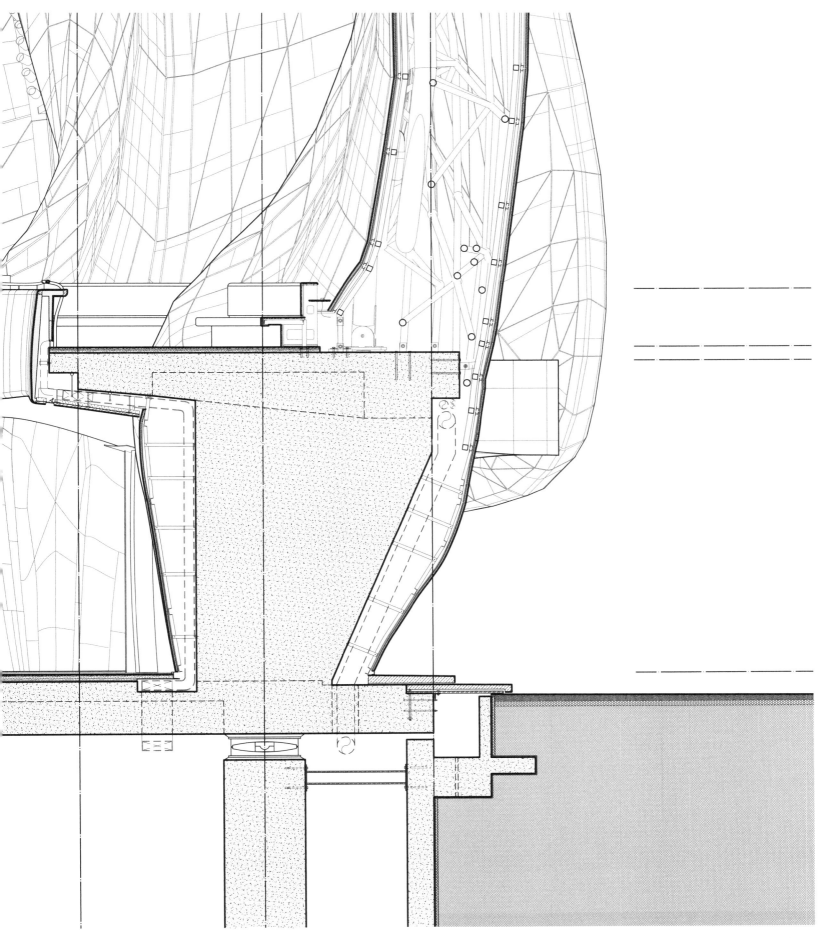

Detail section through column.

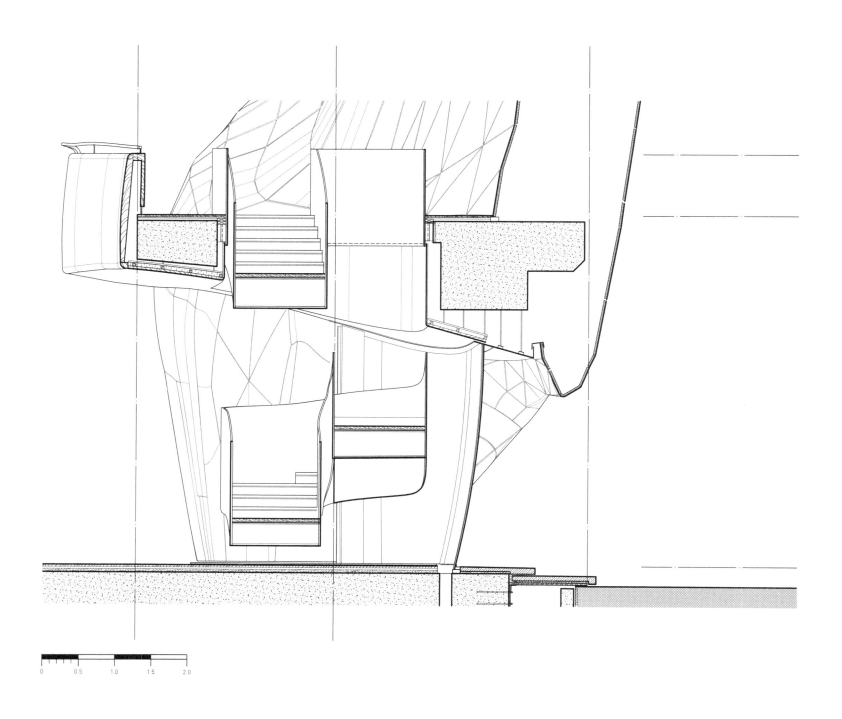

Section cuts through feature stair.

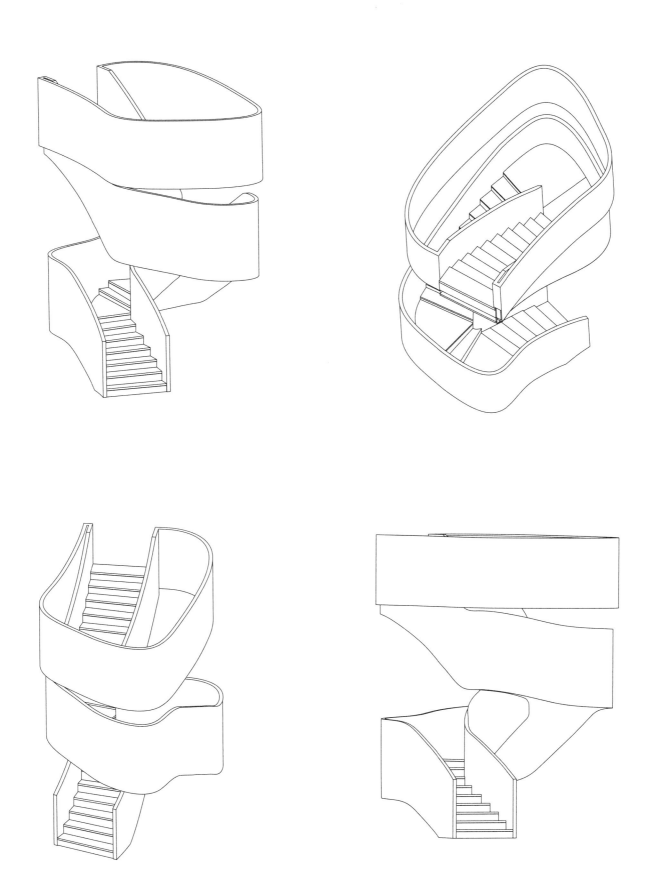

Feature stair axonometrics.

INTERLUDE DEDICATION

THE UNMISTAKABLE LIGHT OF THE WORLD: REFLECTIONS ON THE BAHÁ'Í HOUSE OF WORSHIP IN CHILE

SKY GLABUSH

As we approached the House of Worship through the congested streets of Santiago, it seemed a bit smaller than I had envisioned. On the foothills of the Andes, amidst the pollution, the noise, the smells of the city, it sat nestled in the landscape; a part of the city, but like a visitor awaiting an invitation. Due to the construction, we approached the Temple site obliquely; that is, we entered through the campus of the former boys' school. Greeted by the radiant faces of the volunteers from the Bahá'í community and the surrounding neighbourhood, we were asked, "Would you like to see our trees?" A swimming pool now served as a nursery of sorts. A young volunteer described how these seedlings gathered from the habitat around the temple were part of the 90,000 trees being planted by local volunteers to reforest the area. It is an activity that invites the participation of the residents who live in the vicinity of the Temple grounds; a type of community initiative that draws the local population in. This is not a Temple for Bahá'ís alone. It is an offering to enhance the devotional life of the entire community, in fact, the entire continent, and the pride and enthusiasm with which the volunteers spoke of this undertaking evinced this sense of community and collaboration.

Approaching the Temple from the side, as it were, we walked along a mountain path towards the project management office. Everything was in order, people working peacefully. After a quick visit to the project office, we donned hard hats and set off. Gazing up, the modest and organic image witnessed at the base of the mountain was replaced by a breathtaking crystalline structure shimmering and refracting light, yet nestled in the cradle of the mountains with such majesty and force that it stopped me in my tracks.

> Behold ye that dwell on earth, and ye denizens of heaven, bear witness, He in truth is your Well-Beloved. He it is Whose like the world of creation hath not seen, He Whose ravishing beauty hath delighted the eye of God, the Ordainer, the All-Powerful, the Incomparable![1]

The ascent to the Temple along the slowly arching path, designed for those with restricted mobility, was perfectly paced to allow for just the right amount of time to prepare for what lay ahead. The closer I came within its precincts the more inexplicable it appeared. The exterior structure is infinitely complex but has the purity and simplicity of a magnolia blossom growing out of the rocks and minerals of the arid soil of the mountainside. The combination of absolute wholeness and the torqueing arch of the nine wings that coalesce at the building's oculus sets up a movement, a spinning in the heart. Already reeling with the staggering beauty of the cast-glass cladding, we moved closer. "Enter ye therein in peace, secure."[2]

The moment we crossed the threshold into the inner sanctuary, I lost my breath. I felt as though there was no gravity and I could rise like warm air or smoke. This feeling of a turning and upward-rising motion was like the elation in a dream when you realize you can fly. At this moment when my feet hardly touched the ground I looked over at my fellow traveller to see his reaction.

For Don Rogers, this was the culmination of over a decade of conversations, prayers, trials, and pain that must inevitably accompany an undertaking of this magnitude. The only other time I had seen him so visibly moved was 13 years ago. Our family had just returned from three years in Amsterdam. Julie Rogers and I, with children in tow, were visiting her sister Sasha Rogers, Siamak Hariri's wife, who is a gifted artist in her own right, whose luminous and almost painfully exquisite paintings are in many collections throughout the world and are the crowning element in the Hariri household. The sisters, accompanied by their father, were travelling from Toronto to the Rogers's country home on the shores of Lake Ontario. We stopped at a roadside café and Sasha rose to take a call. When she came back into the diner she said, "Siamak has been awarded the Temple." Watching Don and his daughter Sasha sobbing, surrounded by strangers in a highway coffee shop, was one of those moments that stays with me.

Siamak's relationship to Don is built out of a deep respect, like that of mentor and student, dare I say. Otto Donald Rogers is one of the leading abstract painters in Canada. His art is celebrated for its inventiveness and originality and for the way it blends a material investigation with a deeply poetic and sensitive approach to his religion and faith. So, the ties that bind these two men are familial, artistic, and spiritual. Don's opinion matters, and, according to Siamak, Don had reserved judgment. He wanted to see the building first-hand before weighing in. And it wasn't until entering the Temple that Don understood what Siamak and his team were aspiring to communicate. In his own words:

I had watched the evolution of the architectural concept of the South American Bahá'í Temple from the very early models to the many photographs taken during the construction phases. I felt I had an intimate knowledge of the edifice. I imagined how the interior would be experienced and so when I entered the Temple on my first visit in June 2015 my expectation was to see what was already in my mind's eye. As I crossed the threshold every thought was swept away. I was overcome with tears. My entire being was caught up in a spiral motion, as a prayer being propelled upward toward the Greatest Name of God! This was no longer a building but rather a vision. The North American and the Panama Bahá'í Temples were present at that moment, rejoicing in their joint spiritual enterprise.

Don Rogers recognized that an undertaking of this magnitude is an honour and a bounty that is mysterious. Perhaps, it is rooted in the sacrifices of Siamak's ancestors, and will shed light on future generations. It brings to mind a story that Siamak once shared with me. Below is an account from his relative Gita Ahmanpour:

Our great grandmother's father Qasim and his wife could not have any children. So, he prayed and said to God that if He granted him a child he would contribute gold as much as the weight of the baby and take the money personally to the Holy Land and give it to Bahá'u'lláh. Soon after, they had a daughter, our great grandmother, whom they named Khanum Agha. Qasim, true to his promise, weighed Khanum Agha and took the money to the Holy Land. He told Bahá'u'lláh that he wished to build something for Bahá'u'lláh with his own hands. He was a wealthy man and had many workers who did the building for him, but he wanted to build something with his own hands for Bahá'u'lláh. He ended up building the summer room in Ridván garden. The room that pilgrims go in and pray in. According to our cousin Iraj Mavaddat he and many other of Mavaddat family members stayed there for two years and built a lot of the gardens and structures, including the famous blue and white benches and the fountain in the middle of the Ridván Garden.

When speaking with Siamak years ago he told me that perhaps all the back-breaking labour and concentrated energy that went into the construction of such a building was not the whole story. The reality of its design was perhaps simply a gift, an offering on behalf of his ancestors, "like sweet candy from Heaven." These are stories not often shared. The sacrifices of the early believers of the Bahá'í Faith go untold because of their sincere humility and the sacredness of the family's association with a Manifestation of God.

So, as we entered the building, my initial reaction gave way to a sense of wonder. The inner structure of the Temple is completely infused with light. The panels that line the interior space are made from the most exquisite Portuguese marble with a very fine and subtle graining that is the colour of cream or bleached cotton. This colour is no accident. Siamak spent years looking for the best material to fulfill a vision of a light-infused edifice. The story of how this marble was obtained is itself another stirring tale about families and the effect that past generations have on the present.

For several years, Siamak had been looking for precisely the right marble to line the inner structure of the building. Much of the stone was either too opaque, or, if it was translucent enough, the colour was wrong. Someone had told him of a quarry in Portugal where the stone might be the right colour and translucency. But, even there, he found that the marble was too orange. The owner of the quarry, however, had a special reserve of stone that had been in the family for seven generations. It was something that he would not sell. It was so rare and precious that he was waiting for just the right project. When Siamak described to him the design for the Temple, for the building of the last continental House of Worship, the man realized that he had found the project for which this stone had been waiting.

This Portuguese marble provides the most exquisite quality of light. One or two shades lighter and the illumination would be too intense, like sitting inside a greenhouse, and any darker the light would be dull and opaque. The colour and translucency are perfect, and the walls radiate with a diffused yet concentrated glow.

> A poet is someone
> Who can pour Light into a cup
> and raise it to nourish your
> beautiful parched holy mouth (Hafiz)[3]

The light is familiar and comfortable like the beautiful luminosity that awakens you when camping and the early light appears through the thin membrane of a tent. Or, it is like billowing sails expanding and swelling to catch the air.

> On a day when the wind is perfect,
> the sail just needs to open and the world is full of beauty.
> Today is such a day. (Rumi)[4]

The particular quality of light and the strong upward movement of the central wing-like walls of the building reminded me of a feeling I had as a child. One day our gym teacher took out this enormous white cloth and began to unfurl it across the gymnasium floor. He told us to each take an end and to stretch it out into a perfect circle. "This is a parachute," he said. "On the count of three I want you all to quickly raise the cloth above your head and run underneath." To our utter bewilderment the parachute swelled to its full size and created a spectacular light-filled dome. We all stared at each other in amazement, and all the petty jealousies, private battles, and divisions of exclusive cliques and outcasts had momentarily vanished. We were all together under this blushing orb of cloth. For a brief moment, before the fabric came slowly cascading down on top of us, we were one.

Leaving the House of Worship I wandered around the Temple grounds, still under construction. I could make out the plan for the landscaping and was struck by how perfectly the topography accepted the Temple, how the Andes on one side created a monumental backdrop and on the other the entire city of Santiago was stretched out before it like a twinkling, iridescent carpet. I had seen the Temple many times in photographs and renderings, but nothing prepared me for this first-hand encounter. Where did this design come from?

Siamak was not originally going to submit a proposal. It was his wife Sasha who insisted he do so. Just days before the deadline, he submitted his idea, which was little more than a concept. The simple drawings were of a radiating orb with almost no features. But based on the strength of the idea, and most likely on the strength of Hariri Pontarini Architects' other projects, Siamak's firm made the shortlist[5]. He would be following in the illustrious footsteps of other Canadian architects, such as William Sutherland Maxwell, and Louis Bourgeois, whose masterpiece, the House of Worship in Wilmette, Illinois, served as a locus and inspiration for its counterpart in Chile.[6]

Siamak approached his partner David Pontarini and said, "I want to take a shot at this." David wholeheartedly supported him and Siamak was able to assemble a small team devoted entirely to the realization of a design. They set up a studio in an industrial neighbourhood. Away from the demands of the central firm, they would explore, as never before, the outer limits of their creativity. Siamak asked them to fall backwards, to let go. This period of intense experimentation was risky; it is one thing to imagine a building of pure light, but could it be built? For six months, this nimble team of architects addressed the problem of creating a structure that even challenged the capabilities of two-dimensional design. Bound by some of the restrictions of a Bahá'í House of Worship, namely that it be symmetrical and have nine sides, they began to test the outer limits of the known.

Siamak would conceive certain ideas, and members of his team would attempt to render them as models or as two-dimensional drawings. This process yielded hundreds of small maquettes made from wood, copper, glass, cast plastic, foam, and any number of materials, each striving to translate an extremely abstract vision into form. Only when they began to render ideas into the malleable space of the digital did the concept unfold as a reality. First with Maya, a software used in animation, and then with CATIA, which is used primarily in aerospace engineering, the plan that could now be inverted, flipped, pulled apart and twisted, began to take shape. Drawing inspiration from such ideas as an ancient Japanese woven basket, the flow of the skirt of a whirling dervish, the sloping caress of a cheek bone, the calligraphic matrix of a Mark Tobey painting, the ancient yet modern form of a Bernard Leach pot, these ideas spun around the testing grounds of the uncensored, unbounded creativity of the mind and hand. This type of innovation has at its core a trust that the soul can be inspired, that originality, innovation and inventiveness are gifts received by the receptacle of the heart. The influence of the Divine on the creative process is intrinsic in the Bahá'í Faith and allows for a greater appreciation of the role Siamak Hariri's belief has on his artistic practice. The following Words of Bahá'u'lláh shed light on the origin and source of inspiration:

> Every word that proceedeth out of the mouth of God is endowed with such potency as can instill new life into every human frame, if ye be of them that comprehend this truth. All the wondrous works ye behold in this world have been manifested through the operation of His supreme and most exalted Will, His wondrous and inflexible Purpose. Through the mere revelation of the word "Fashioner," issuing forth from His lips and proclaiming His attribute to mankind, such power is released as can generate, through successive ages, all the manifold arts which the hands of man can produce.

This, verily, is a certain truth. No sooner is this resplendent word uttered, than its animating energies, stirring within all created things, give birth to the means and instruments whereby such arts can be produced and perfected.[7]

As people from around the world come into contact with this sacred structure, the generating influence of these Words will be demonstrated in the precise equilibrium of innovation and tradition, of craft and experimentation, of fastidious detail and warm, inviting hospitality, of order and dreamy flights of the imagination. At its heart, this building is simple, yet it is also at the leading edge of technology. It is essentially modern but without the emphasis on the ego and the superfluous flourishes of contemporary design that convey a kind of spectacle of materialistic branding. It is modern in the sense of being truly new. Indeed, ʼAbduʼl-Bahá, Baháʼuʼlláhʼs Son and the Authoritative Interpreter of His Words, states that true modernity is the renewal of religion. Let me conclude with His soaring and illuminating Words that cut to the heart of the matter, Words that capture the spirit and essence of this precious and bedazzling achievement:

The ocean of divine mercy is surging, the vernal showers are descending, the Sun of Reality is shining gloriously. Heavenly teachings applicable to the advancement in human conditions have been revealed in this merciful age. This re-formation and renewal of the fundamental reality of religion constitute the true and outworking spirit of modernism, the unmistakable light of the world, the manifest effulgence of the Word of God, the divine remedy for all human ailment and the bounty of eternal life to all mankind.[8]

1 Shoghi Effendi, *World Order of Baháʼuʼlláh* (Chicago: US Baháʼí Publishing Trust, 1991), p. 104.
2 Quran, 15:46.
3 Hafiz, *The Gift: Poems by Hafiz, the Great Sufi Master,* translated by Daniel Ladinsky (New York: Penguin Compass, 1999), p. 8.
4 Rumi, *Love Poems from God: Twelve Sacred Voices from the East and West,* translated by Daniel Ladinsky (New York: Penguin Compass, 2002), p. 57.
5 Notable early projects are McKinsey & Companyʼs Toronto headquarters (the youngest building in the city to be granted heritage status), the MacLaren Art Centre in Barrie, Ontario, and numerous private buildings that resonate with exceeding confidence, acumen, and a rare sense of scale and proportion.
6 The Canadian connection goes further than this. Vancouverʼs Fariborz Sahba designed the Lotus Temple in New Delhi, India. Also, Canadian-Iranian Hossein Amanat designed the Seat of the Universal House of Justice, The International Teaching Centre, and the Centre for the Study of the Sacred Texts on Mount Carmel, Haifa, Israel.
7 Baháʼuʼlláh, *Gleanings from the Writings of Baháʼuʼlláh,* pp. 141–142.
8 ʼAbduʼl-Bahá, *Foundations of World Unity* (Chicago: Baháʼí Publishing Trust, 1979), p. 9.

THE DAWNING PLACE OF THE REMEMBRANCE OF GOD: FROM VISION TO REALITY

ROBERT WEINBERG

Well, I dream'd
That stone by stone I rear'd a sacred fane,
A temple, neither Pagod, Mosque, nor Church,
But loftier, simpler, always open-door'd
To every breath from heaven, and Truth and Peace
And Love and Justice came and dwelt therein[1]

This longing for the raising of an edifice that would encourage the purest form of religious devotion was first published in 1892, in the final collection of verse by Britain's great Victorian Poet Laureate, Alfred, Lord Tennyson (1809–1892). Here Tennyson conceives of religion as a wide embrace, unmarred by conflict, exclusivity, or man-made differences. In that same year, just a few months before the poet's death in the south of England, another notable figure passed away in the remote Ottoman penal colony of Acre on the eastern edge of the Mediterranean. Most probably unbeknown to Tennyson, the Founder of the Bahá'í Faith, Mirzá Husayn-'Alí (1817–1892), known as Bahá'u'lláh (Arabic: "The Glory of God"), had endured four decades of incarceration and harsh banishment at the hands of powers determined to extinguish his influence and the remarkable religious movement he had brought into being. Despite the probable lack of connection between these two luminaries — separated by some 3,500 kilometres and the paucity of reliable contemporary accounts that might have further enlightened the poet — one might today perceive in Tennyson's yearning a sensitivity to the very spirit of the age that Bahá'u'lláh's followers believe was released into the world with the advent of his Revelation.

At the heart of this Revelation was the recognition of the essential unity of all things. Bahá'u'lláh described how the spiritual seeker who had arrived at this conception of reality "looketh on all things with the eye of oneness, and seeth the brilliant rays of the divine sun shining from the dawning-point of Essence alike on all created things, and the lights of singleness reflected over all creation."[2] Thus Bahá'u'lláh proclaimed the existence of a "primal oneness deposited at the heart of all created things."[3] With that recognition comes the acknowledgement of the oneness of God, the oneness of religion, and the oneness of humanity.

Bahá'u'lláh taught that, throughout history, an essentially unknowable Divine Creator has made known its will and purpose through a succession of inspired educators — or Manifestations of God — each of them possessing the same authority and carrying out the common mission of renewing timeless spiritual truths while instituting new laws and teachings to remedy the ills, and meet the exigencies, of the age in which they appear.[4] Such teachings should not merely be considered as the profound thoughts of a brilliant, human mind; rather they represent nothing less than Divinely-endorsed aims, inherently imbued with the power to realize their purpose.

Advancing the weighty claim to be the latest of these Manifestations of God, Bahá'u'lláh laid out for society a pattern in which gender, racial, religious, class, and all other forms of prejudice and divisiveness would eventually cease to exist. It was a message that he had expressed in person, some two years before his passing, to the distinguished Cambridge orientalist Professor Edward Granville Browne, alone among Westerners to be granted a series of interviews with this prisoner of Acre. Browne conveyed, through a unique pen-portrait, the profound impression made upon him by one whom he described as "the object of a devotion and love that kings might envy and emperors sigh for in vain."[5]

"We desire but the good of the world and the happiness of the nations; yet they deem us a stirrer up of strife and sedition worthy of bondage and banishment," Bahá'u'lláh told Browne. "That all nations should become one in faith and all men as brothers; that the bonds of affection and unity between the sons of men should be strengthened; that diversity of religion should cease, and differences of race be annulled — what harm is there in this?"[6]

Yet, for such a vision to be realized, lofty aspirations and good intentions alone would not be adequate. In scores of volumes of writings, Bahá'u'lláh not only expounded upon universal values and principles, but also promoted habits and practices for the individual and society, specifically ordaining and designing institutions that harmoniously blend the spiritual with the temporal administration of human affairs. Through such means, he averred, humanity might attain its collective maturity and establish and sustain a long-hoped-for era of peace and prosperity.

Among such institutions, 'Houses of Worship' should be erected, "throughout the lands in the name of Him Who is the Lord of all religions."[7] Defined in Arabic as *Mashriqu'l-Adhkár* ("Dawning-place of the remembrance of God"), these Temples would open their doors to all. "Then, with radiance and joy, celebrate therein the praise of your Lord, the Most Compassionate,"[8] instructed Bahá'u'lláh. Within the century and a half that followed its birth, the Bahá'í Faith spread to every country on the planet, and such "sacred fanes" of which Tennyson dreamed began to appear on continent after continent as expressions of the oneness of God and religion.

In broad terms, the *Mashriqu'l-Adhkár* is defined as any building — in a city, town, or village — that is dedicated to the praise of God. Specifically, however, Bahá'u'lláh envisaged a new structure of society where the life of a community, inspired and motivated by the highest values, would begin each day with the recitation of, and reflection upon, the revealed Scriptures of the world's great religious traditions. Daily worship in the Temple, established at the spiritual and physical heart of community, would then be translated and transfused into service to the surrounding society. To this end, essential dependencies would emerge, situated around the House of Worship, each of them dedicated to social, humanitarian, educational, and scientific pursuits.

Every morning, in the serene atmosphere of the House of Worship's central auditorium, the sacred verses of the world's great religions would be read or sung, freed from any practice that distracts from the pure power of the revealed Word. Thus in the Bahá'í Temple, there are neither rituals nor ceremonies; no iconography, statuary, pulpits, sermonizing or interventions by a clergy; nor collections of money.

At other times of the day, the House of Worship's doors would be open, inviting all to come for private prayer and meditation. To emphasize this inclusivity, a small number of architectural elements are specified in the writings of the Bahá'í Faith: that the building should be circular in shape and have nine entrances.[9] The only symbol on display inside the auditorium is a calligraphic rendering in Arabic of the phrase "O Thou Glory of the Most Glorious," positioned at the exact centre at the apex of the building.

New Modes of Expression

The example of Tennyson's response to the spirit of the age encompasses the notion that, whenever a Manifestation of God appears in the world, the impact of his Revelation is felt far beyond his own orbit and those who physically hear the message or respond directly to his call. The lives and works of these unique beings release creative forces that can subliminally affect hearts and minds further afield and set in motion wider processes of change. Percy Bysshe Shelley (1792–1822) expressed such an idea in his declaration that poets are "the hierophants of an unapprehended inspiration, the mirrors of the gigantic shadows which futurity casts upon the present, the words which express what they understand not; the trumpets which sing to battle, and feel not what they inspire..."[10]

The insatiable appetite for experimentation and ceaseless search for meaning among artists, writers, architects, and composers throughout the late-nineteenth and twentieth centuries; their challenging of time-honoured values and traditions; and their quest for new modes of expression — all of these phenomena might be understood as the activities of a world whose equilibrium has been upset by the forces released by a renewed Divine message. In nature, the rising of the sun each day provokes a physical response to its life-giving radiance and is welcomed by a cacophony of sound and activity. In similar manner, the steady ascent of a luminous new vision of a human race that is collectively coming of age would no doubt make an impact upon the souls of those who are sensitive to its influence. As a result, the Bahá'í writings suggest that the peoples of the world are being unknowingly propelled through the turbulence of adolescence, inexorably moving towards a maturity in which the reality of their unity will be recognized, while their infinite diversity will be upheld and celebrated.

For this reason, in these early days of the evolution of a truly universal consciousness, it would be premature to claim that there could be such a phenomenon as Bahá'í art or Bahá'í architecture. When the American painter Mark Tobey (1890–1976) — whose exquisite "white writing" abstractions have been cited as an influence by the architects of the House of Worship in Santiago — met with Bahá'u'lláh's great-grandson and then Guardian of the Bahá'í Faith, Shoghi Effendi (1897–1957), he was told that there could be no such thing as "Bahá'í art" at this stage in the Faith's development.[11] A religion must give rise to a new model of society, and indeed civilization, before finding its highest expression in art forms that could be said somehow to be fully representative of its history, teachings, and values. For Tobey, this was a great liberation; a set of beliefs that had no iconic tradition enabled him to visualize Bahá'í concepts freely and develop his own pictorial expression, without feeling that he was bound to convey ideas in a prescribed or restricted way. In like manner, the architects of the Bahá'í Houses of Worship thus far erected around the world have been given the freedom to find their own language to express the fundamental concept of unity that such a building represents. This has given rise to a range of approaches and styles that are at once diverse yet connected, rooted in — but not bound by — the architectural traditions of the past and the discoveries of the present, while fully employing the unprecedented opportunities offered by technological innovation.

Continental 'Mother Temples'

During the twentieth century, as the Bahá'í community's membership expanded and spread globally, a program gradually unfolded to establish the *Mashriqu'l-Adhkár* around the world, commencing initially with the building of one House of Worship on each continent. These became known as continental 'Mother Temples.'

The first House of Worship was completed in 1908 in Russian Turkistan. Under the protection and freedom granted by the then Russian authorities, more than 1,000 Bahá'ís escaped persecution in their homeland of Iran and settled in the city of 'Ishqábád (now Ashgabat, Turkmenistan). For the first time anywhere, a true Bahá'í community came into being, with its own *Mashriqu'l-Adhkár* complex — including House of Worship, a travellers' hospice, schools, medical clinic, and other facilities. In terms of its architectural features, this Temple largely reflected the prevalent Islamic culture of the region. After being expropriated by the Soviet authorities and turned into an art gallery, the House of Worship was severely damaged in an earthquake and eventually demolished in 1963.

The oldest surviving Bahá'í House of Worship stands on the shores of Lake Michigan in Wilmette, Illinois, USA, north of Chicago. After the cornerstone for the Temple was laid in 1912 by Bahá'u'lláh's son and appointed successor, 'Abdu'l-Bahá (1844–1892), the building took some four decades to complete, requiring new technologies to bring the vision of its architect to fruition. To this day, the 'Mother Temple of the West,' as it is known, remains entrancing in its beauty and inventive decoration. Clad in white Portland cement concrete with both clear and white

1. First Bahá'í House of Worship; Russian Turkistan (now Ashgabat, Turkmenistan); completed 1908, demolished 1963; Ustad 'Ali-Akbar Banna Yazdi.

2. Mother Temple of the West; Wilmette, Illinois, U.S.A; 1953; Louis Bourgeois.

3. Mother Temple of Africa; Kampala, Uganda; 1961; Charles Mason Remey.

4. Mother Temple of Australasia; Sydney, New South Wales, Australia; 1961; Charles Mason Remey with John Brogan.

1

2

3

4

6

7

5

8

9

5. Mother Temple of Europe; Langenhain, Germany; 1964; Teuto Rocholl.

6. Mother Temple of Latin America; Panama City, Panama; 1972; Peter Tillotson.

7. Mother Temple of the Pacific Islands; Apia, Samoa; 1984; Hossein Amanat.

8. Mother Temple of the Indian Subcontinent; New Delhi, India; 1986; Fariborz Sahba.

9. Bahá'í Temple of South America; Santiago, Chile; 2016; Siamak Hariri.

quartz aggregate, the House of Worship appears to capture light, its exterior, lace-like tracery incorporating carvings of a variety of the world's sacred symbols. The Wilmette House of Worship was a particular inspiration to the architects of the present Temple in Santiago, who envisioned their 'Mother Temple of South America' as a sister to its North American counterpart.

Two further Houses of Worship were dedicated in 1961 — the 'Mother Temple of Africa' in Kampala, the capital of Uganda, and the 'Mother Temple of Australasia' near Sydney, Australia. Less architecturally ambitious than the edifice in Wilmette, both of these buildings nevertheless mirror its basic structure with an entrance level auditorium forming the base for a middle level drum, crowned by a dome. Both Temples appear to blend quite naturally into their surrounding environs, encircled by beautiful gardens of rare and native plants, which enhance the environment and the atmosphere of spirituality.

In 1964, the 'Mother Temple of Europe' near Frankfurt, Germany, was dedicated. Altogether more modernist in its conception, the House of Worship is made of steel, aluminum, and glass, and stands perhaps as a stylistic reflection of the industrialist, reconstructive mood of post-World War II Germany. Removing the central drum feature of previous Houses of Worship, its architect enlarged the dome to sit directly atop the ambulatory and auditorium level, and perforated it with 540 diamond-shaped windows that allow for the diffusion of sunlight into the central hall, creating an ethereal quality and an exceptional acoustics.

The Bahá'í House of Worship in Panama City, Panama, opened in 1972. It serves as the 'Mother Temple of Latin America.' Overlooking the city, perched on a high cliff known as "Singing Hill," the Temple is constructed of local stone laid in a pattern reminiscent of Native American fabric designs. Naturally evolving from the ground level and dome conception of the European House of Worship, this Temple is open to the elements, welcoming the passing breeze and birds. This openness is also a feature of the 'Mother Temple of the Pacific Islands' in Apia, Samoa, completed in 1984. The building was dedicated by Malietoa Tanumafili II (1913–2007), the first reigning Bahá'í head of state.

The monumental 'Mother Temple of the Indian Subcontinent' was completed in New Delhi, in 1986. Inspired by the ancient symbol of the lotus flower, its design is composed of 27 freestanding, marble-clad 'petals' arranged in clusters of three to form nine sides. One of the most visited buildings in the world, the House of Worship has won numerous architectural awards and has been the subject of countless articles in the press and media.

The 'Mother Temple of South America' takes the design of Bahá'í Houses of Worship one stage further; the entire building is essentially a dome that encapsulates and rises above the central prayer hall. While interpreting the brief for such buildings, it is as if Hariri Pontarini Architects have moved entirely away from any other existing building as a point of reference, creating a form that is as unique, integrated, and whole as the teachings and aims it represents.

With the opening of the House of Worship in Santiago, the Bahá'í community's program of constructing such buildings at the continental level is complete. The next stage of the realization of Bahá'u'lláh's vision, the creation of national and local Houses of Worship, is now under way in particular parts of the world where the size of the Bahá'í population and its work in local community development has evolved to such a point that the need for a *Mashriqu'l-Adhkár* becomes evident; the construction of the institution is a fruit of growth and societal transformation. Plans are already being executed to erect the first two National Houses of Worship in Papua New Guinea and the Democratic Republic of Congo, and five local Houses of Worship in localities in Cambodia, Colombia, India, Kenya, and Vanuatu. In essence, these buildings are a gift from the Bahá'ís of the world to humanity, funded entirely by the voluntary financial contributions of the followers of Bahá'u'lláh, wherever they may reside.

In his *Kitáb-i-Aqdas* ("Most Holy Book"), Bahá'u'lláh called for the Bahá'í House of Worship to be "as perfect as is possible in the world of being."[12] In their design, function, beauty, and refinement, the Temples are a physical reflection of the harmony of spiritual truth, as well as a vehicle by which the power that the Word of God possesses to transform human hearts and behaviour can be made accessible to many, inspiring a new pattern of life. In the care and spirit embodied in every detail and element of these buildings, one might sense an echo of the words of another contemporary of Bahá'u'lláh's, the British art critic and commentator John Ruskin (1819–1900):

Therefore when we build let us think that we build forever. Let it not be for present delight, nor for present use alone; let it be such work as our descendants will thank us for, and let us think, as we lay stone on stone, that a time is to come when those stones will be held sacred because our hands have touched them, and men will say as they look upon the labour and wrought substance of them, "See! this our fathers did for us."[13]

1 Alfred, Lord Tennyson, "Akbar's Dream" in *The Death of Cenone, Akbar's Dream and Other Poems* (London: Macmillan & Co, 1892).
2 Bahá'u'lláh, *The Seven Valleys and the Four Valleys* (Wilmette, Ill.: Bahá'í Publishing Trust, 1986), p. 18.
3 'Abdu'l-Bahá, *Selections from the Writings of 'Abdu'l-Bahá* (Haifa: Bahá'í World Centre, 1978), p. 263.
4 Manifestations of God mentioned in the Bahá'í writings include Adam, Moses, Abraham, Krishna, Zoroaster, Buddha, Jesus Christ, Muhammad, The Báb, and Bahá'u'lláh.

5 Edward G. Browne, cited in Hasan Balyuzi, *Bahá'u'lláh, The King of Glory* (Oxford: George Ronald, 1980), p. 372.
6 Edward G. Browne, cited in Hasan Balyuzi, *Bahá'u'lláh, The King of Glory* (Oxford: George Ronald, 1980), p. 373.
7 Bahá'u'lláh, *The Kitáb-i-Aqdas* (Haifa: Bahá'í World Centre, 1992), K. 31, p. 29.
8 Bahá'u Bahá'u'lláh, *The Kitáb-i-Aqdas* (Haifa: Bahá'í World Centre, 1992), K. 31, p. 29.
9 Nine is the numerical value for the word Bahá' ('Glory') in *Abjad* notation, in which each letter of the Arabic alphabet is assigned a specific numerical value. Nine

is also the highest single digit, signifying unity.
10 Percy Bysshe Shelley, quoted in Donald Reiman and Sharon Powers, ed. *Shelley's Poetry and Prose* (New York: W. W. Norton, 1977).
11 Marzieh Gail, *Other People Other Places* (Oxford: George Ronald, 1982), p. 201.
12 Bahá'u'lláh, *The Kitáb-i-Aqdas* (Haifa: Bahá'í World Centre, 1992), K. 31, p. 29.
13 John Ruskin, *The Seven Lamps of Architecture* (New York: John Wiley & Sons, 1860), pp. 142–3.

DEVELOPMENT TEAM

Client
The National Spiritual Assembly of the Bahá'ís of Chile
The National Spiritual Assembly of the Bahá'ís of Canada

Client Representative
Mashiyat Ashraf

Project Management
Desarrollo y Construcción del Templo Bahá'í de Sudamérica Ltda.

Architect
Hariri Pontarini Architects
Partner-in-Charge: Siamak Hariri
Project Manager: Doron Meinhard
Project Architect: Justin Huang Ford
Project Team: Michael Boxer, George Simionopoulos, Tiago Masrour, Táhirih Viveros, Rostam Sohaili, Jin-Yi McMillen, Jaegap Chung, Adriana Balen, John Cook, Mehrdad Tavakkolian, Donald Peters, Jimmy Farrington, Miren Etxezarreta-Aranburu, Jeff Strauss

Local Architects
BL Arquitectos S.A.
Project Lead: Klaus Georg Benkel Opitz and Pablo Larraín Marshall
Pablo Luna Arquitectos
Project Lead: Pablo Luna

Landscape Architect
Juan Grimm
Project Lead: Juan Grimm
Project Team: Marcella Benítez, M. Catalina Yaconi D.

Structural Consultants
Halcrow Yolles (CH2M HILL)
Project Lead: Chris Andrews
Project Team: Crispin Howes, Bill Coupe, Li Ming Tang (Carruthers & Wallace)

Sirve S.A.
Project Lead: Juan Carlos de la Llera
Project Team: Emiliano Pinto, Paula Silva

Patricio Bertholet M. Ingeniería Estructural
Project Lead: Patricio Bertholet M.
Project Team: Christian Cuevas

VMB Ingeniería Estructural
Project Lead: Leopoldo Breschi
Project Team: Ian Watt, Angel Aragón, María Jesús Aguilar

Structural and Cladding Consultants
Simpson Gumpertz & Heger
Project Lead: James Parker
Project Team: Glen Bell, Frank W. Kan, Amy Hackney, Graham Cranston,
Jennifer Williamson, Russell Davies, Casey Moore

Mechanical, Electrical, HVAC, Civil Consultants
MMM Group
Electrical Project Lead: Kevin Cassidy
Mechanical/HVAC Project Lead: Craig Watson
Civil Project Lead: Mani Ruprai
Project Team: Jorge Elias, Tony Chan, Alex Lui, Brian Van Bussel, Emiliano DeLemos,
Shahriar Saeed-Pour, Pejman Khodarahmi, Andrea Counsel, Mike Nitescu

The OPS Group
Project Lead: Gunnar Heissler

Videla & Asociados/DICTUC S.A.
Project Lead: Eduardo Melgarejo
Project Team: René Guerra, Ramon Lobos

CR Ingeniería
Project Lead: Cipriano Riquelme, Marcelo Riquelme
Project Team: Sergio Zurbero

GHD
Project Lead: Alfredo Grez
Project Team: Eduardo Gonzalez, Karla Gonzalez

Elektrica
Project Lead: Didier Gonzalez

Lighting Consultants
Limarí Lighting Design Ltda.
Project Lead: Pascal Chautard
Project Team: Carolina Roese, Raul Osses González, Cristina Fahrenkrog,
Francisca Nicoletti

Isometrix Lighting Design
Project Lead: Arnold Chan
Project Team: Eduardo Gonzalez, Karla Gonzalez

Acoustics
Absorbe
Project Lead: Veronica Wulf

Way-Finding/Graphics
Entro Communications
Project Lead: Udo Schliemann
Project Team: Sofie Nilsson

Chilean Legal
Grupo Vial Serrano Abogados
Project Lead: Manuel José Vial Vial
Project Team: José Miguel Olivares, Sergio Guzmán, Vanessa Pinto

Vergara Galindo Correa Abogados
Project Lead: Eduardo Correa Martínez

Civic Administration
Municipalidad de Peñalolén
Project Lead: Claudio Orrego
Project Team: Marisol Rojas

Additional Consultants
Acapulco Pools, Aqua-plans, Bascuñán y Maccioni, ECE Group, Excel Projects, GRed Ingeniería, ImperGes Chile, IngeSmart, INTRAT Consultores S.A., Itai Bar, Journey Freight, LRI, Marisol Rojas (Asenta), Mauricio Poblete y Cia LTDA., Pro-Bel, Simonetti y Cia., TROW/EXP, Vermeulens Cost Consultants

CONSTRUCTION TEAM

Project Management
Desarrollo y Construcción del Templo Bahá'í de Sudamérica Ltda.
Project Lead: Saeid Samadi, Enayat Rohani
Project Team: Samira Rahimi, Carl Ewing, Felipe Parra, Javier Duhart, Alejandra Guauque, Jorge Tapia, Seena Samimi, Anís K. Sadeghpour, Natalie Nia, Tiago Masrour, Táhirih Viveros

Superstructure and Cladding
Josef Gartner GmbH
Project Lead: Stefan Zimmermann
Project Team: Armin Franke, Klaus Knebel, Bernd Ruf, Thomas Kuhn, Jens Wendel, Rostam Sohaili, Günter Burkhardt, Michael Sendelbach, Sebastian Utz, Dimitry Demin, Ulrich Stadelmann

Glass Casting
Jeff Goodman Studio
Project Lead: Jeff Goodman
Project Team: Sylvia Lee, David Williamson, Evan Butters

Contemporary Glass Design Ltd.
Project Lead: Vladimir Fridman
Project Team: Michael Fridman

Stone Fabrication
EDM, Ateliers de France
Project Lead: René Camart
Project Team: Emmanuel Mormede, Eduardo Soares, Guillaume Gomez, Pierre Frey, Pascal Guitet, Matthieu Gerard, Clement Lorrain

Owen Sound Ledgerock
Project Team: Tom Stobbe, Justin Weber, Jenna Thomson, Lynda Grimoldby, Rob Jolley, Joe Ryckman

Wood Fabrication
Merritt Woodwork
Project Lead: Michael Merritt
Project Team: Keith Merritt, Mark Mantione, Albert Peetoom, Dennis Scott, Jennifer Rolfe

Concrete Superstructure
Fernandez Wood Constructora S.A.
Project Lead: Alex Wömpner

Ancillary Buildings/Hardscape
Constructora Jorge Carrasco Farías S.A.
Project Lead: Rodrigo F. Reyes S.

Landscaping
Jardín Bora Bora

Local Support/Stone Installation
Gleixner y Gleixner

Road Infrastructure
Constructora Fapisa S.A.
Project Lead: Rodrigo F. Madrid S., Constanza Quintana Manzo

Additional Contractors/Collaborators
Accurate Models & Prototypes, Age of Bronze, Audio Musica, Carlos Medina,
Constructora Alvial S.A., CR Ingeniería e Instalaciones Térmicas LTDA., Engineered
Lighting, Earthquake Protection Systems, Excel Projects, Farahbakhsh Youssefi,
Filo Timo, Francisco Gazitúa, Geocom, Global Spectrum, H+A, Home Control,
Lummel GmbH, Mariani Metal, Mewes Aduanas, New Season Woodwork, NüProtec,
PMC, Proyectos Mantención y Construcción LTDA., RHI AG

Although the above list acknowledges the contributions of many, an undertaking of
this complexity could not have been possible without countless others. We would like
to offer our sincerest thanks to all those who offered their time and efforts in order to
realize this project.

In addition, we would like to acknowledge all of the people who worked tirelessly
to realize this publication, including: Andreas Müller, Justin Huang Ford, Udo
Schliemann, Joseph Cho, Stefanie Lew, Mell Furs, Kevin Boothe, Jun Khang, Heike
Strempel, and Katja Jaeger.

Hariri Pontarini Architects (HPA) is a full-service Canadian firm devoted to producing work of lasting value for their clients. Siamak Hariri and David Pontarini founded the Toronto office in 1994, motivated by a shared commitment to design quality. Today their 120-person practice offers its clients in-depth partner involvement through all stages of design and the breadth of building experience and technical expertise to rigorously oversee construction. HPA believes solid relationships result in strong projects. They take pride in forging lasting collaborations with all involved in the design, development and construction process. With each commission, HPA assumes full responsibility to materialize a design vision inspiring to its occupants, attuned to its setting, and respectful of stakeholder needs, client budget, and timeline. Every project in their diversely scaled, award-winning portfolio reflects the HPA mission to craft architectural and urban solutions that exceed expectations, without excess. In 2013 HPA won the Royal Architectural Institute of Canada's Architectural Firm Award.

Siamak Hariri is a founding Partner of Hariri Pontarini Architects. His portfolio of nationally and internationally recognized buildings has won over 60 awards, including the Governor General's Medal in Architecture. In 2016, he was celebrated as one of Canada's Artists who mattered most by *The Globe and Mail*.

One of Siamak's earliest projects, the Canadian headquarters of McKinsey & Company is the youngest building to receive City of Toronto heritage landmark designation. Since then he has established a career creating institutional and cultural projects of international acclaim, including the Governor General's medal winning Schulich School of Business for York University and the Richard Ivey School of Business at Western University that has been recognized with the 2016 Chicago Athenaeum International Architecture Award, the American Institute of Architects' Educational Facility Design Award of Excellence, and the Lieutenant Governor of Ontario's Award for Design Excellence in Architecture.

More recent public and private projects include the international competition winning Jackman Law Building, Faculty of Law for the University of Toronto, the Weston Family Learning Centre at the Art Gallery of Ontario, the multi-phase Welcome Project for the Royal Ontario Museum, the recently completed award-winning Casey House, and the new Tom Patterson Theatre for the internationally renowned Stratford Festival.

Born in Bonn, Germany, Siamak was educated at the University of Waterloo and Yale University where he completed a Master of Architecture. He has taught at the Daniels Faculty of Architecture, Landscape and Design at the University of Toronto, as well as been a lecturer and guest critic for numerous organizations across North America. Siamak was recently awarded an Honorary Doctorate of Architecture from Ryerson University for his contribution to architecture in Canada and abroad. Siamak lives in Toronto with his artist wife, Sasha Rogers, and their three children — Lua, Yasmin, and David.

ABOUT THE CONTRIBUTORS

Sky Glabush lives and works in London, Ontario, where he teaches studio art at Western University. He holds a Bachelor of Fine Arts from the University of Saskatchewan and a Master of Fine Arts from the University of Alberta. Recent exhibitions include "The window is also a door" at Prosjektrom Normanns in Stavanger, Norway, "What is a self?" at Oakville Galleries, "The Kingdom of Names" at Thames Art Gallery, and "The Visible and the Invisible" at the Art Gallery of Windsor. Glabush's work is in many public collections including the Canada Council Art Bank, McIntosh Gallery, Museum London, Mackenzie Art Gallery, Mendel Art Gallery, and the Bank of Montreal. He is married, with four children, and is actively engaged in community-building initiatives with the Bahá'í community.

Douglas Martin is a historian by training. He served for 12 years on the Universal House of Justice, the international governing council of the Bahá'í world community, after serving as the Director of the Office of Public Information at the Bahá'í World Centre. For more than two decades, he was also the Chief Executive Officer of the National Spiritual Assembly, the governing council of the Bahá'ís of Canada.

Lisa Rochon is a champion of aspirational design and livable cities in Canada and around the world. She is an author, public speaker, and curator, serving as a leader on design juries. As *The Globe and Mail's* award-winning architecture critic (2000–2013) she wrote about architecture from her base in Toronto, and reviewed transformative architecture in a diversity of cities, including Dhaka, Mumbai, Medellin, Paris, and New York. A Senior Fellow at the University of Toronto's Global Cities Institute, Lisa is a graduate of Sciences Po, Paris, and holds a Master of Arts (Urban Design Studies) from the University of Toronto.

William Thorsell served as Editor-in-Chief of *The Globe and Mail* (1989–1999) and Director and CEO of the Royal Ontario Museum (2000–2010). He is a visiting fellow at the Munk School of Global Affairs, University of Toronto, and serves on various non-profit boards in Toronto.

Robert Weinberg is a UK-based broadcast journalist and radio producer. He is the author of 10 books covering aspects of Bahá'í history, as well as classical music and art. From 2009 to 2013 he served as Director of the Bahá'í International Community's Office of Public Information, based in Haifa, Israel. He is currently a member of the National Spiritual Assembly of the Bahá'ís of the United Kingdom.

IMAGE CREDITS

Hariri Pontarini Architects: 12, 16, 18, 21, 25, 34/35, 42/43, 46, 48–59, 62/63, 74/75, 78–85, 102/103, 110–123, 126/127, 128/129, 130/131, 140, 142–155, 158/159, 166/167, 175, 177, 179, 181, 183, 185, 187, 198/199, 202/203, 204, 206/207, 208/209, 210–219, 252

Ian David: 44

Juan Grimm: 86–88, 91

Siamak Hariri: 15, 19, 20, 24, 48, 49

National Spiritual Assembly of the Bahá'ís of Chile: 174, 176, 178, 180, 182, 184, 196/197

Office of External Affairs, Templo Bahá'í: 192/193

Jean Roux: 27

Nabil Sami: 61, 94/95

Ruth Shafa: 226/227

Simpson Gumpertz & Heger: 117

Raul Spinasse: 224/225

Benjamin Straub: 93

Guy Wenborne: 30/31, 36/37, 38/39, 76, 106/107, 108, 125, 134/135, 136/137, 162/163, 172, 186, 189, 190/191, 194/195, 200/201, 236

Sebastián Wilson León: 2/3, 4/5, 10, 29, 32/33, 40/41, 64–73, 96–101, 104/105, 132/133, 138/139, 157, 160/161, 164/165, 168–171, 221, 222/223, 228–235

Every reasonable attempt has been made to identify owners of copyright. If unintentional mistakes or omissions occurred, we sincerely apologize and ask for a short notice to the author. Such mistakes will be corrected in the next edition of this publication.

Book design: Binocular, New York
Production: Katja Jaeger, Heike Strempel
Paper: 150 g/m^2 Amber Graphic, 170 g/m^2 Garda Gloss
Printing: DZA Druckerei zu Altenburg GmbH

Library of Congress Cataloging-in-Publication data
A CIP catalog record for this book has been applied
for at the Library of Congress.

Bibliographic information published by the German
National Library

The German National Library lists this publication
in the Deutsche Nationalbibliografie; detailed
bibliographic data are available on the Internet at
http://dnb.dnb.de.

This publication is also available as an e-book
(ISBN PDF 978-3-0356-0722-2)

© 2018 Birkhäuser Verlag GmbH, Basel
P.O. Box 44, 4009 Basel, Switzerland

Part of Walter de Gruyter GmbH, Berlin/Boston

Printed on acid-free paper produced from chlorine-
free pulp. TCF ∞

Printed in Germany

ISBN 978-3-0356-0847-2

9 8 7 6 5 4 3 2 1   www.birkhauser.com